Help, Lord!
I'M HOSPITALIZED

GLORIA HAMER

Daybreak Books
Zondervan Publishing House
Grand Rapids, Michigan

Help, Lord! I'm Hospitalized.
Copyright © 1989 by Gloria Hamer

Daybreak Books
are published by
Zondervan Publishing House
1415 Lake Dr., S.E.
Grand Rapids, MI 49506

Library of Congress Cataloging-in-Publication Data

Hamer, Gloria.
    Help, Lord! I'm hospitalized / by Gloria Hamer.
      p.   cm.
    ISBN 0-310-51481-9
    1. Sick—Prayer-books and devotions—English. 2. Hospital
patients—Prayer-books and devotions—English. I. Title.
    BV4910.H36   1989
    242'.4   1989   89-31523
                                                        CIP

Unless otherwise noted, Scripture quotations are taken from the *Holy Bible: New International Version* (North American Edition), copyright © 1973, 1978, 1984 by the International Bible Society. Used by permission of Zondervan Bible Publishers.

NAMES IN THIS BOOK HAVE BEEN CHANGED TO PREVENT IDENTIFI-CATION, EXCEPT FOR THE AUTHOR'S.

Edited by Anne Severance and Nia Jones

Printed in the United States of America

90   91   92   93   94 / CH / 10   9   8   7   6   5   4   3   2

DEDICATION

To my loving husband, John, an unfailing source of encouragement. During my siege with neuromuscular illness, he has become a world-class shopper and errand runner.

To our daughter, Amy Kathleen, and son, Brian John. Blessings from God, they are a source of pride and joy.

To my mother, Elaine Johnson Gordon, who has faithfully reported for active duty during my chronic illness no matter where we are living. To visit us in Michigan, this brave Hoosier boarded a dilapidated commuter plane which later threatened to shake apart mid-flight. (If necessary, she would have borrowed Air Force One.) Taking command of our post, she laundered, cooked, baked, and scrubbed appliances more times than I care to admit in print.

Most importantly, this book is dedicated to Jesus Christ my Savior, who has sustained me during numerous hospital stays and eight years of sickness. He has strengthened my faith, preserved my sense of humor, and blessed me richly. As I wrote this book I often prayed, "Father, I don't know what to say, but you can use me to inspire others with your Word. Help, Lord."

EPIGRAPH

Thinking about going to the hospital is about as delightful as anticipating a prison sentence. We don't want to go! When we become patients, we cope with skimpy gowns, embarrassing procedures, and roommate conflicts. Disturbers of the peace appear in throngs. Worries multiply: Will my surgery be successful? How is my family managing without me? Will I be able to go back to work? Will I ever feel healthy again?

Thanks be to God for we are not alone. Our heavenly Father upholds us with his mighty arm. As we enter the hospital to battle illness and disability, may we remember the Lord's promise to Joshua, "Do not be terrified; do not be discouraged, for the LORD your God will be with you wherever you go" (Josh. 1:9).

Contents

I FEEL LIKE I'VE LOST CONTROL OF MY LIFE.

"For I know the plans I have for you," declares the LORD, "plans to prosper you and not to harm you, plans to give you hope and a future."

JEREMIAH 29:11

I would have preferred a weekend at a plush resort, but here I am in this hospital. In what seemed like endless admitting procedures, I answered grueling questions and proved that I have adequate funds to pay the bill (in gold nuggets, if necessary). Later an ID band was snapped in place on my wrist and I was wheeled to an assigned room (complete with strange roommate), where I was ordered to disrobe. I stepped into a scanty hospital gown, climbed into bed, and modestly pulled the sheets up to my chin.

Now so many people are trooping in and out of my room that I feel as if I'm scheduled for a press conference any minute. Asked for "donations," I oblige with several vials of blood and a urine specimen.

It's time to play "Twenty Questions" with the

staff. Some of the questions seem so absurd that I suspect this is a mind game to test my frustration level. I am teased by such thought-provokers as: "How old was your maternal grandmother when she developed her first wart?" And another that I've asked myself dozens of times already: "Why are you here?"

My weight, blood pressure, pulse, and temperature are recorded on a mysterious medical chart— mysterious because I'm not permitted to see the results. (I'm tempted to appeal to my congressman. I'll bet I could get better answers from him!) The bed controls are so confusing that I almost crush my pelvis between the portable metal tray and the rapidly rising bed.

I checked in five hours ago. I want to go home.

When illness strikes, patients experience a wide range of emotions. We may feel anger toward the disease or circumstances that triggered the hospitalization. We may even be mad at the physician for insisting on the admittance. We're anxious and confused too. Hospitalization is a rude interruption in our routine.

Do you remember how you felt the last time you were caught in a traffic jam? Perhaps there had been an accident, and all lanes were paralyzed. You, like every other driver behind the wheel, had a destination in mind, maybe even a critical deadline to make. Nevertheless, there you sat, slumped over the steering wheel, unable to budge. Did you feel anger? Frustration? Did your blood pressure rise? Maybe you felt like shaking your fist and blasting your horn as some of the other drivers were doing, but did their temper tantrums have any effect on the situation? Of course not. Only when the lanes were finally cleared did the flow of traffic resume.

Illness is like being caught in a traffic jam—everything in life comes to a screeching halt. We make plans with the expectation of carrying them out, but when sickness or surgery interrupts, we feel as if we have lost control. Like the irate motorists stalled by the wreck on the interstate, we check our watches and grumble, "I'm tired of this hospital, of this delay. Let's get moving!"

Dick, a corporate executive, felt this kind of anxiety when he was hospitalized with kidney stones. He snapped at the volunteers, argued with the surgeon, and, more than once, threatened to dress and walk out.

To understand Dick's behavior we need to examine his normal routine. On the job this energetic forty-year-old supervises dozens of employees and oversees the operation of a huge office complex. Dick is accustomed to "calling the shots."

In the hospital, though, he was no longer in command. Dick felt robbed of his privileges. He was told when to eat, what to eat, what to wear, and when he could entertain visitors. In strange and frightening surroundings, he was dependent on doctors, nurses, and medications. He handled his anxiety by masking his fears behind a tough veneer. The truth is he ached for the familiar. More than anything, Dick yearned to be sitting in his swivel chair at the office, organizing details and barking orders.

We're all basically cut from the same fabric as this frustrated executive. We may not have positions of authority, but we like to think we can control our own destiny.

The book of James cautions us against taking such an attitude. Oh sure, we make plans for the future. Our calendars might be clogged with social and business obligations for the next eight months. But the clincher is the question: "Will our plans actually come to fruition?" James reminds us that we don't know what tomorrow will bring. He adds, "What is your life? You are a mist that appears for a little while and then vanishes" (4:14).

To what does he compare our lives? A mist. Some would find this comparison insulting. After all, who wants to think of himself or herself as no more significant than the steam cloud forming over a boiling tea kettle! James, of course, is not saying that we have no value. We are of priceless worth to our heavenly Father. Rather, James uses this illustration to point out the brevity of our earthly lives when measured against eternity.

How foolish we must appear to the angels who look down upon us as we zip across interstates and race to beat the clock. What's the hurry? Good question. Illness is an appropriate time to ask ourselves: Where am I going? Why am I in such a rush to get there? We'll come back to these questions later.

James continues in this passage by suggesting that we amend our plan-making to include six crucial words: "If it is the Lord's will." We might say, "If it is the Lord's will, I'll get well and return to my job." "If it is the Lord's will, when this surgery is behind me, I'll accept that promotion and move to the East Coast." "If it is the Lord's will, I'll go back to college and get my degree."

Only God knows the outcome of all our careful planning. Our knowledge is so limited we don't even know how many days we will spend on this planet. In contrast, our Creator knows the exact number of birthdays we will celebrate. In fact, even before we were conceived, God recorded those days in his Book (Ps. 139:16).

Most of us plan and save for the "golden years," but we could fall victim to a stroke, heart attack, kidney failure, or any other disease long before retirement. This body provides temporary housing, at best.

As our plans fall by the wayside, we will endure heartaches and suffer bitter disappointments. What does our Lord say to us about the future? In Jeremiah 29:11 he assures us that he has plans for us—not evil plans—but plans to give us hope and a future. Even when life seems to crumble in around us, God is shaping and molding us for his kingdom. Our hopes are set on Jesus, our Redeemer.

When we sing "Jesus, Savior, pilot me," we picture him at the helm of a ship. Sometimes we stubbornly seize control and insist on navigating our own way. But what happens when we take over? We may change course, arriving at the wrong destination. Or we may venture onto the rocks and capsize.

Let's relinquish the captain's chair permanently,

resting in the assurance that we will stay afloat only so long as he is at the controls.

Where are we going? Ultimately we are headed for eternity. God has promised to steer us safely to this final destination. When is our scheduled arrival? Only he knows, but we will pass through heaven's gate not one minute sooner nor one minute later than expected.

Let's relax and enjoy the trip.

Father, this illness was not a part of my plans. Dealing with the unexpected makes me feel helpless and "out of control." Help me to acknowledge your omnipotence. Enable me to yield my will to yours and give up this power struggle once and for all. May I, by your grace, fulfill the plans you've made for my future. In Jesus' name I pray. Amen.

ROOM 415, BED 2: AM I JUST A NUMBER?

"I have summoned you by name; you are mine." : ISAIAH 43:1

*I*n the busy atmosphere of a hospital, it is easy to feel like a nonentity—"the kidney stone in bed one" or "the appendectomy in bed two." If you have been admitted for tests, you may feel like a white rat undergoing bizarre experiments. You worry that you might even forget your own name.

Like some of you, I experienced a mild "identity crisis" while hospitalized. For an entire month I underwent dozens of tests. Each morning I winced when I heard a wheelchair or cart being shoved through my door by an aide. It was obvious that I was about to be transported elsewhere. Common sense told me that we wouldn't be heading for the snack bar!

For each adventure I struggled into my robe and slippers and mounted my "chariot." Next we sprinted toward the appropriate testing area. Upon arrival I was neatly lined up against one wall behind several other patients slumped in wheelchairs. In single file, we all faced north. For several minutes or even hours we obediently waited for our turn to "be in pictures."

Finally it was my chance to provide the entertainment. My body was contorted into twisted shapes that I was to "hold." Then I was x-rayed, twirled, rotated, or bariumed, depending upon the mood of the technician.

Each time the picture crew finished "shooting," I was wheeled to the hallway and efficiently lined up against the opposite wall in single file. Finally a volunteer bounced toward me, checked something on my chart, and whisked me back to my floor. *I feel like a piece of U.S. mail,* I thought. *First I'm intake and then I'm output. Maybe I'm just junk mail. No one speaks to me. People just read my chart.*

I often felt like I had been "lost in the shuffle," but this feeling peaked just before my surgery when an incredible mix-up occurred. I had been properly prepped and pre-opped and was lying on a gurney— groggy, but not yet asleep. It was a blessing that a remnant of consciousness remained!

An intern floated toward me and commented, "You sure are allergic to lots of medications."

"Just sulfa," I mumbled.

He frowned. "Joyce? Are you Joyce?"

I was instantly alert. "I'm Gloria!" My thoughts raced. *Who is Joyce? Is she having something put in, taken out, or altered? If the surgeon operates on me, thinking I'm Joyce....*

My thoughts were interrupted by the young man at my side. "I'll be back. Better see what's going on here."

After a few minutes he drifted toward my bed again. "I did some checking. There was a mistake on the surgical roster. We thought you canceled, but everything is straightened out now. Don't worry about a thing."

I surrendered reluctantly to sleep, only half convinced that I would get the proper operation.

Maybe I should not have shared that experience with you. You might be tossing your clothes in a suitcase right now, ready to dash for home. Relax. This type of incident seldom occurs.

But like me, I'm sure you're feeling the need of proper recognition. It's easy to feel like so many pounds of flesh in a nameless body. Does it upset you when staff members are so engrossed with their duties that they fail to address you by name?

And what do you really think of that scanty little number you're wearing? Hundreds of men, women, and children are dressed just like you. We patients must model faded, thin cotton gowns that seem to have twice as many openings as closings. These garments are neither fashionable nor distinctive.

At such frustrating times it is comforting to read again Jeremiah 1:5: "Before I formed you in the womb I knew you." Think of that—God knew us before we were conceived. Our existence was no accident, but a part of his divine plan. You and I were created by a loving Father *who knows our names*!

God cares for us even though we are riddled with sin. He knew we would never attain perfection so he sent Jesus, his Son, to live the perfect life for us. That same Jesus hung on the cross at Calvary for our sins. We need not dread death because it has no power over us. Through faith in Christ we are conquerors.

In Revelation 3:5 we read, "He who overcomes will, like them, be dressed in white." We will never again wear these abominable hospital gowns. Instead, we'll be wearing Designer originals, robes of righteousness washed clean and white in the blood of Christ. In them we'll stand before the throne of God, our voices blending in a mighty chorus of praise and worship to the King of Kings.

As believers our names are listed on something far more important than a medical chart. Our names are written in the Book of Life, recorded there before the foundation of the world. Jesus reminded his followers in Luke 10:20: "Rejoice that your names are written in heaven." What cause for celebration!

Imagine it. Reservations for heaven. We will stroll upon streets of gold and fellowship with all the saints who died knowing Christ as Savior.

In eternity we will have no need for canes, wheelchairs, oxygen tanks, and dialysis machines. No one will attach identification bracelets to our wrists or herd us toward examination rooms and testing booths. Sickness will have ended forever. Our frail, earthly bodies will be transformed into glorified bodies that can't feel pain or grow old and infirm. How marvelous!

Yes, you and I are very special. We are V.I.P.'s. Let's rejoice that the Good Shepherd calls us by name.

Heavenly Father, it's humiliating to be treated like a part of a human assembly line. How grateful I am that you will never think of me as a nameless face in the crowd. Why, you know me so intimately that you can discern my thoughts. Thank you, Lord, that my name is already written in the Book of Life. I am important because I belong to you. In Jesus' name I pray. Amen.

MANY ARE THE DISTURBERS OF MY PEACE.

"Peace I leave with you; my peace I give you. I do not give to you as the world gives."

JOHN 14:27

*H*ospital sounds compose a unique, unfinished symphony. Feet provide the rhythm section as they alternately shuffle, march, or pad softly down the long, narrow corridors. Orchestral voices include intercom messages, blaring televisions, ringing telephones, and squeaky surgical carts. A snoring bunkmate punctuates the melody at predictable intervals.

Add considerable instrumentation if your bed is near an area being remodeled. You'll clench your teeth to the pounding of the hammer and the grinding of electric drills. What confusion! What discord! Anyone for an aspirin?

As we all know, sick people are supposed to get plenty of rest. In a hospital, though, this is next to impossible. In addition to coping with the constant noise, patients face other stresses. For example, you may feel that your privacy is being violated. Again and again. Just think for a moment about the number of people—mostly strangers—who enter your room at will. This "cast of thousands" includes the cleaning crew, doctors, surgeons, nurses, newsboys, visitors, interns, chaplains, volunteers, and repairmen. And always there is a steady stream of vampires seeking blood. Yours!

You may feel like you are hosting some sort of Open House. This feeling intensifies during formal visiting hours when friends and family arrive in throngs. Why, your bunkmate might even hold an informal family reunion, with second cousins draped over your chairs and perched on the end of your bed!

And you? You're feeling miserable. Your smile wore out after that last injection. Besides you have to go to the bathroom. How embarrassing to ask everyone to leave so you can call the nurse for a bedpan. So you suffer in silence, fighting the urge to pull the sheet over your head and hide until they're gone.

After surviving a challenging day, you assume that since night is coming, you'll finally get some rest. Not necessarily. It's true that fewer people will flow in and out of your room, but the sounds will continue unabated. Voices and machines will "serenade" you throughout the evening hours.

Allow me to insert a personal experience that occurred when I was a patient at No Mercy Hospital. Around midnight I was awakened by loud voices. I was shocked to see a strange man in nightclothes being escorted from my room. The confused fellow took issue with the staff but his mumbled words were too soft for me to discern. This is what I did hear from the nurse:

"What are you doing out here in your pajamas, Mr. Jones?" Mumble, mumble. "No, Mr. Jones. *This is not your room.* Your room is down the hall. Let me help you find it. Ah, here we are. Now what?" Mumble, mumble. "Yes, I know there's a man in that bed. He's your roommate. Now here's *your* bed. Lie down and *please* go to sleep, Mr. Jones."

I was relieved when Mr. Jones was tucked into the proper bed. I would have appreciated having a lock on my door!

I trust you will never undergo a similar experience. It is possible, though, that you were sleeping soundly while such an encounter took place outside *your* room.

So what are you going to do about your own lack of privacy? You could tack a NO ADMITTANCE sign on your door, but no one would pay any attention to it. Besides, the people who come in and out of your room have a good reason for doing so. They are not collecting items for a rummage sale nor participating in a scavenger hunt. They're there to serve you.

Face it. You will get precious little privacy until you are dismissed. You may choose to spend the rest of your life as a hermit, but for now you'll need to tolerate the unpleasant situation. Maintain your sense of humor and invest in an inexpensive set of earplugs if necessary. Catnap whenever possible. Most important of all, seek that which soothes the soul.

Corrie Ten Boom knew where to turn for peace and restoration in an era that caused many less stalwart souls to lose their grip on reality. The daughter of a Holland watchmaker, Corrie was shoved into the back of a truck during World War II and herded into a concentration camp. Prisoners were crowded together in flea-infested barracks. Guards were cruel and food was scarce. The women were forced to sleep huddled together.

Nevertheless, as she endured unspeakable horrors in captivity, Corrie had a sense of peace that radiated from her. A strong believer, she had stored God's Word in her heart and it served her well. She had discovered what she called "the hiding place." In the camp this devout woman shared her secret with other prisoners in the hope of leading them to Christ. God's Word was Corrie's source of strength. The Nazis may have been successful in ripping her from her home, family, and possessions, but no one could rob her of God's promises. She knew the Lord was watching over her.

God loves you and does not want you to be anxious and troubled. His message? "Be still, and know that I am God" (Ps. 46:10). The Lord of Hosts, who created the heavens and the earth, will take care of you. If you are a child of God, if your sins have been forgiven through Jesus Christ (Rom. 5:1), you need not worry about the future. You will one day dwell in the presence of the Lamb.

Even in the midst of confusion and upheaval, Christians can listen for the "still, small voice." We need not be shaken by disastrous events. We can live above chaos. Even though our ears are bombarded by every kind of noise, our hearts can be flooded with peace. Not a peace that the world gives or comprehends, this inexhaustible peace flows from the heart of our heavenly Father. Let's draw on it.

Dear Lord, it all gets to me sometimes—the clamor, the uncertainty, the lack of privacy. Oh, how I ache to go home. Grant me strength and courage to endure. I choose to focus on you, Father, and your promise of peace. I claim that now and always. In his name. Amen.

HOW CAN I SERVE GOD HERE?

"Go into all the world and preach the good
news to all creation."

MARK 16:15

S uddenly you are a missionary. That's right, a missionary! Oh, don't worry. You won't have to give up ice cream, nor will you have to learn how to keep a battle-worn jeep in good repair. Forget about the passport, mosquito netting, clothing barrels, and Bible translations. Yours is a local mission station. You already have all the equipment you will need.

It may be hard to believe, but many people who enter your hospital room have never heard the gospel. No doubt they're familiar with space shuttles, VCR's, popular recording artists, and the most highly rated television shows. They might even know which colors look best with their particular skin tones. Sadly, though, many of them are ignorant of spiritual matters. If asked "Where will you spend eternity?", these folks may fumble for an answer. That may be exactly why God has brought you to this mission post!

You've probably read stories about David Livingstone, the famous missionary to Africa, who dedicated his life to God's service. His exciting adventures are chronicled in encyclopedias and library books. But the missionaries I want to talk about here have never set foot on foreign soil. You won't find any books written about them, nor have they been written up in *Who's Who*. Nevertheless, they have drawn many others to Christ during their unique ministries of illness.

Let's talk about Jane Ellen, a bright eight-year-old with jet black curls and a pug nose. This charming, precocious girl fell victim to leukemia years before much was known about treating this illness. Jane Ellen spent most of her second-grade year in St. Mary's Hospital, keeping up with her school lessons with the help of a tutor.

With her pleasant, sunny attitude, Jane Ellen spread joy to those who ministered to her. Her unwavering faith was a source of strength. She never hesitated to ask visitors and staff if they believed in Jesus. Why? Because she wanted to be sure that her family and friends would be joining her in heaven someday.

As Jane Ellen's condition deteriorated, doctors gave up hope for her survival. When her distraught parents wept in her presence, Jane Ellen attempted to comfort them. "Please don't cry, Mommy and Daddy. Jesus is coming for me soon now and then I'll be well. All the pain will be gone. No more shots and treatments. Try to be happy for me. Please!"

Within the week a small coffin cradling Jane Ellen's body was lowered into a freshly dug grave. Scores of friends—young and old—attended the services along with family members. Today her parents still remember how mourners expressed their feelings about this child: "She was an inspiration. Her faith was incredible. This girl's testimony means so much to me." Janie's witness lingers on like a pleasant fragance to those of us who were blessed by her short life.

Like Jane Ellen, Bill Lucas is a faithful missionary. Bill's life changed drastically one gray November morning as he traveled to work. A sleeping driver approaching from the opposite direction veered across the center line and slammed his car into Bill's station wagon. For the next few weeks Bill's life hung in the balance as he struggled to recover from broken bones and severe internal injuries. One badly mangled leg had to be amputated.

Each time his wife sat by his bed in the Intensive Care Unit, she read Scripture aloud to him. At first Bill showed no response. Days later he slowly whispered to his wife, "Whether we live or die, we belong to the Lord." He had memorized Romans 14:8 as a young man, but now the verse took on a brand-new meaning. As a Christian, Bill knew he couldn't lose. If God willed it, he would live and cope with new limitations. If not, he would join his Savior.

To the amazement of all his physicians, Bill survived. Today he is confined to a wheelchair, but what a radiant witness! All who visit him, including his minister, come away refreshed and encouraged. Bill is grateful that his life was spared and is eager to share what God has done for him. "I'm just so glad to be alive," Bill says. "Each day is like a gift. You know, I now see things I never even noticed before. I really have many reasons to thank the Lord."

Jane Ellen and Bill took up their crosses and followed the Master. Despite physical afflictions, they obeyed Christ's command to "go into all the world and preach the good news to all creation" (Mark 16:15). These "Hospital Bed Evangelists" have worked just as diligently in their fields as any missionary who serves thousands of miles from his or her homeland.

You and I are equipped as missionaries too. Every believer has access, through prayer, to the helmet of salvation and the sword of the Spirit (Eph. 6:17). As members of the body of Christ we are commissioned to proclaim Christ to the whole world. Without faith in Jesus, people in darkness will perish in their sins. We have great news for them. Scripture says, "How beautiful are the feet of those who bring good news!" (Rom. 10:15).

The apostle Paul was a splendid example of a faithful missionary. Even while jailed, he sang praises to God and wrote uplifting letters to the churches. His mission station at the time was a prison! But this ambassador for Christ wasn't shy about preaching "on location." Whether he was worshiping in a temple, sailing on a ship, visiting in a home, walking along a road, or appearing by summons to appear in the Governor's auditorium, Paul was always quick to testify that Jesus is the Son of God.

How can you and I serve God from our hospital beds? Here are a few suggestions:

1. We can fill ourselves with the Word of God

daily, storing up God's promises and memorizing special passages.

2. We can be prayer warriors, praying for our families, friends, church, nation, the hospital staff, and others.
3. If we can hold a pencil and paper, we can write uplifting letters and notes to others undergoing trials, sharing how God has blessed and sustained us through health difficulties.
4. We can listen to others as they unburden their problems and let them know that we care. More importantly, we can assure them that God cares.
5. We can develop a joyful attitude in spite of our physical afflictions. Let's not be disheartened by chemotherapy treatments, intravenous tubes, or oxygen tents. Beyond this trial, exquisite joy awaits the believer.

Those who are hospitalized have been granted a unique opportunity. We can reach out with God's love to as many people as possible. Though we may feel trapped by our circumstances, maybe even view our bodies as prisons, let's look through the bars and rejoice that the Word of God remains unfettered. We can advertise that good news wherever we go, making wise use of this precious time to witness to the glory of God.

Dear Father, I get so wrapped up in my own troubles that I tend to forget about others. I'm grateful to be among the redeemed. Help me to recognize the unique opportunities I have for witnessing in this place. Prompt me to report to "active duty" as your missionary. In Jesus' name. Amen.

I NEED A ROOMMATE TRANSPLANT.

"We love because he first loved us."

1 JOHN 4:19

*H*ospital roommates can be hazardous to your health! If you doubt that statement, just ask yourself the following:

Has your blood pressure risen unexpectedly since admittance to the hospital?

Do you suffer from unexplained headaches?

Are you tempted to hitch a ride on a laundry cart so you can escape from your room?

If you answered in the affirmative to any of the above, you will be encouraged to learn that all of these bizarre symptoms will disappear (a) when you are dismissed from the hospital, or (b) when you get a different roommate!

Let's face facts. When two strangers are paired arbitrarily in a hospital setting, conflicts are bound to occur. Why, at this very moment you may be sharing a room with a person who plays the television from dawn to midnight—at ear-splitting decible levels. On the other hand, you may be rooming with an insomniac. If so, you already know that some insomniacs become quite animated in the middle of the night. They clip their toenails, rearrange closets, play solitaire, or hum a favorite show tune. Is it any wonder that you feel sicker now than when you were admitted a few days ago?

During my own numerous hospitalizations, I have logged time with virtually every type of roommate, including a coarse woman I can't forget. She swore at the staff, threatened to sue everyone but the chaplain, and burped so loudly that the reverberations could be heard in the hall.

Most of my companions, though, had one thing in common. They were Olympic-competition conversationalists. Especially Edith. Allow me to introduce you to her. Edith, a sixty-year-old divorcée, quit her secretarial position because of her disability. She and I bunked together in a sprawling university hospital many miles from both of our homes. I enjoyed talking with her, but not "non-stop." I wanted private time to read or write in my journal. In contrast, Edith rarely paused for breath.

One day, when I couldn't handle her perpetual chatter any longer, I hobbled out of bed and pulled together the orange-striped curtain separating us. I wanted to be sure that Edith could not see me. Then I told a white lie: "I'm going to take a nap now."

I smiled triumphantly as I snuggled between the sheets and cautiously plucked my spiral notebook and a novel from my nightstand. I turned each page slowly and quietly. But apparently not quietly enough.

Within minutes Edith's high-pitched voice sliced the air. "Gloria? Gloria? Are you awake already?"

I winced. "Well, uh. . . . "

"Oh good. Now, as I was saying. . . . "

Even though the curtain was pulled shut, Edith continued her monologue, rambling on until our supper trays arrived hours later. My slow burn fanned into a blazing rage. *I can't get a thing done for this woman's incessant talking!* I fumed. *Why in the world did I have to get her for a roommate?*

That October evening I was grateful when sleep finally put an end to Edith's marathon talking spree. For a while I reveled in the peace and quiet. But after my evening devotions, I began to compare Edith's life with my own. I had a beautiful family, a loving husband, and many supportive Christian friends. On the other hand, my talkative roommate had precious little. She was crippled by a debilitating disease and lived in a bleak, two-room apartment. Alone. Her husband hadn't been able to handle her illness and had divorced her shortly after the diagnosis. All she had was a cat. A cat and a television set.

I was suddenly ashamed. *No wonder she can't stop talking. This is probably the first time she's had human companionship in a long time. She actually seems to be enjoying this adventure.* Then I prayed, *Dear Lord, give me a better attitude toward this lonely woman. Give me opportunities to witness to her and to show her your love.*

God gradually changed my selfish attitude. The next morning I deliberately questioned Edith about her life during the Great Depression. She shared with me the tragic circumstances that led to her father's suicide and its effect on her family's struggle to survive. I found myself truly caring for Edith as a person.

Days later she surprised me by asking questions about God and the Bible. Edith was not aware that Christians can be absolutely certain they are going to heaven when they die. Each time she asked me a theological question, I thumbed through the Bible and read the answer aloud. "I'm so relieved," she sighed. "I never knew what was in the Bible before. Now I'm not afraid."

As you might have guessed, a friendship developed between the two of us. When we were released from the hospital, we exchanged letters for years until Edith's recent death. I miss her. How grateful I am that she touched my life.

What kind of roommate dilemma do you face? What are some possible solutions? You must consider your own physical and emotional health, of course, and make the decision that is best for all concerned. So don't feel guilty if you need to request a transfer to another room. In certain situations this action will be necessary to eliminate added stress.

Much of the time, however, forgiving Christians can coexist with almost any type of roommate. Some suggestions for survival include the following:

1. Pray for your roommate. Try to see that individual through Jesus' eyes. After all, he died for that person, too.

2. Ask God for patience and flexibility as you try to adjust to a stranger's habits and routines.
3. Vent your feelings in a journal. Writing helps release tensions.
4. Don't forget that this situation is temporary. You and your companion may never have future contact.
5. Develop a sense of humor about the situation. Write to a friend and share something funny or peculiar about your hospital stay. Look for opportunities to laugh. Laughter reduces stress and enables us to focus on something other than illness and tests.
6. Pray for opportunities to witness. As you read your Bible during personal devotions, for example, your roommate might notice and ask questions.
7. Read daily the love chapter in First Corinthians 13. God gives us the power to love and, in fact, commands us to do so.

We who are hospitalized can, with God's help, make the best of our situations. Above all, let us continue to witness for him, "hold[ing] out the word of life" (Phil. 2:16).

Father, forgive me for my selfishness. Broaden my narrow vision to include this roommate, who is suffering too. Thank you, Lord, for your continued love and strength. In Jesus' name. Amen.

WHY, LORD? WHY ME?

"Blessed is the man who perseveres under trial, because when he has stood the test, he will receive the crown of life that God has promised to those who love him."

JAMES 1:12

R ick, a thirty-seven-year-old accountant, discovered during his hospitalization that he had a rare blood disease that does not respond to any known treatment. Rick was shocked by the diagnosis. When his clergyman strolled into the room for a visit, Rick pounced on him. "Why?" Rick demanded. "Would you please tell me why God is doing this to me? I've tried to do the right thing. I go to church and take care of Judy and the kids. Pastor, tell me why this is happening!"

Jennifer was an only child, born to a couple in their late forties. Eighteen years later, during a routine exam, the doctor discovered a strange-colored mole on Jennifer's arm. Tests indicated it was malignant melanoma. Because the cancer cells had already begun to race through her body, this gifted young woman was given only months to live. She and her grieving parents pleaded with God. "Why? What have we done to deserve this tragedy?"

Ruth, the mother of two preschoolers, is afflicted with a disease of the connective tissues—lupus erythematosus. She requires frequent hospitalization and is often unable to care for her children. She doesn't look sick, but wrestles with pain, reduced stamina, and other complications of this serious illness. Sometimes Ruth struggles with depression. She feels God has singled her out for "punishment," and claims, "I could cope better if I knew why God gave me this disease."

Rick, Jennifer, and Ruth blame God for their illnesses. When faced with adversity they—like so many of us—ask, "Why, Lord?" Pastors say that suffering Christians wrestle with this question more than others. Believers often feel that God must be punishing them. Consequently, they struggle to pinpoint which past or present sins have caused the Almighty to "turn against them."

What do you think? Does God punish us for our sins by sending us physical or emotional affliction? Scripture assures us, "God was reconciling the world to himself in Christ, not counting men's sins against them" (2 Cor. 5:19). As sinners we merit God's wrath, but we escape because of Jesus' blood. "God made him who had no sin to be sin for us, so that in him we might become the righteousness of God" (v. 21). Can you believe it? We are counted righteous!

So now you're suffering and there are many unanswered questions. Is God really all-powerful? If so, where was he when you fell victim to this sickness?

Doubts invade your mind. Maybe you aren't as important to God as your coworker who hasn't been sick a day in his life. Why, come to think of it, that colleague isn't even a Christian, yet enjoys excellent health. You are puzzled. None of this makes sense.

A certain believer from the ancient city of Uz was blameless and upright, yet he suffered more than you or I can possibly imagine. I'm talking about Job, of course. Job feared and loved the Lord, but he encountered incredible trials anyway. He lost his children, his cattle, and ultimately his health. Even his wife coaxed him to "curse God and die" (2:9). Did he? No. "In all this, Job did not sin in what he said" (v. 10).

Was Job distressed? Sure. He mourned. He even cursed the day he was born. As he squatted in the ashes, scraping loathsome boils with a piece of broken pottery, he looked so miserable that his so-called friends didn't recognize him when they paid a sick call.

No one spoke a word for a whole week because Job's suffering was so intense. Oh, how much better it would have been if these three men had just kept quiet. When they did venture to say something, they blamed Job for his predicament. Some comfort!

Job finally responded bluntly, "Miserable comforters are you all!" (16:2). Scorned by his colleagues, plagued with painful sores, and grief-stricken with loss, Job also had a nagging wife. Nevertheless, he continued to honor God: "I know that my Redeemer lives, and that in the end he will stand upon the earth. And after my skin has been destroyed, yet in my flesh I will see God" (19:25–26).

Job had vertical vision. He could look beyond his

present anguish to what was coming. With unflagging certainty he believed in the Resurrection. He knew Christ would rescue him from his mortal body and lead him through the gates of heaven. That promise gave him hope. No matter how bleak his circumstances, he knew he could depend on the deliverance of God.

Instead of viewing our own situations with despair, let's draw encouragement from Job's example of faith and perseverance in the midst of tribulation. Christians are not granted a merry "exempt status" from suffering.

We might ask, "Why is the world in such a mess anyway?" Paul answered that question in Romans 5:12: "Sin entered the world through one man." Adam and Eve sinned when they disobeyed God by eating of the Tree of Knowledge of Good and Evil, and God mercifully cast them out of Paradise. Had they tasted the fruit of the Tree of Life, the couple would have lived forever in misery. Because of their sins the ground was cursed and the pain of childbirth was greatly multiplied.

As long as you and I live on this earth, we are candidates for heartbreak, loneliness, accidents, and a host of physical and emotional ailments. We would have preferred for God to have run interference, blocking us from trouble. He didn't choose to do so. Why? That question is one of life's mysteries. We creatures cannot understand the mind of our Creator. "For my thoughts are not your thoughts, neither are your ways my ways, declares the LORD" (Isa. 55:8).

What next? Can we trust God? Of course we can. He is in control of the universe and has unlimited power and knowledge. Let's stop insulting him by asking, "What have I done to deserve this?" Christ took our punishment for sins on that blood-soaked cross. Illnesses are hazards of living on this earth. If God permits sickness to enter our lives, let's trust him to accomplish his purposes through it. He can use our afflictions to his glory.

What does God say about troubles? "Blessed is the man who perseveres under trial, because when he has stood the test, he will receive the crown of life that God has promised to those who love him" (James 1:12). Though it may stretch your imaginative powers a bit, could you possibly begin to think of your illness as a blessing? I realize that you wouldn't (while of sound mind) pick surgery as a favorite pastime. How, then, are we blessed? We are blessed because we learn a deeper trust in the Lord as we lean on him, claiming his power and strength.

We can claim, "My comfort in my suffering is this: Your promise preserves my life" (Ps. 119:50). Notice that the last word is *life*, not *death*. That sums up the Christian's hope. We are promised a crown of life when our earthly journey ends.

Rick, Jennifer, Ruth, and all who trust in God as Redeemer have reason to rejoice. Our trials on this earth may be overwhelming, but we will not be overcome. Deliverance is on the way. It's a promise!

Father, I've shouted toward heaven, demanding to know why this tragedy has twisted my plans and saddened my life. I won't pretend that I like it. Besides, you already know my heart. But with your help I will put the "Why me?" questions behind me and trust you for the future. Take away my nearsightedness and enable me to see beyond this present pain to that which is eternal. In his name. Amen.

MY FAMILY NEEDS ME AT HOME.

"When anxiety was great within me, your consolation brought joy to my soul."

PSALM 94:19

*E*veryone knows that mothers aren't supposed to get sick. When they do, the family unit may threaten to self-destruct. Now some of you aren't mothers and never will be. Let's face it. Some of you are men! This hospitalization is stressful for you too. Perhaps you feel that you are neglecting your family or your job. Your spouse is pinch-hitting for you on the home front and is swamped with added responsibilities, such as a leaky water heater or broken furnace.

If you are a single parent, you're really in a bind. Neighbors and family are probably watching the kids, and you had to opt out of carpooling until further notice. This lousy hospital stay has wreaked havoc with your plans and the plans of others. You aren't exactly thrilled to be a patient. In fact, you sometimes struggle with guilt.

I know the feeling. During my hospitalizations I

often felt guilt-ridden along with my other symptoms. The illness wasn't my fault. After all, none of us is blessed with an indestructible body. Even so, I felt that I was abandoning my family.

For example, shortly after I was admitted to Methuselah Memorial Hospital, my phone rang. I answered.

"Mom?" came a small voice.

"Yes, honey. How are you?"

"Okay. I just got home from school. Mom, when are you coming home?"

I had been at the hospital for less than two hours. My maternal instincts told me I should dress and go home even if I died in the process. Wisdom dictated that I stay put. Wisdom prevailed. I stammered, "Well, the doctor thinks I won't be here over two or three days."

"That's what you said last time. You were gone a month."

"I know. I'm sorry. Maybe this time I won't have to stay so long."

"I wish you could come home. Now!"

I hung up with the certainty that I would not be nominated as Mother of the Year. Yes, phone calls from home can definitely pile the guilt on a patient. Mothers are especially susceptible to "Telephone Terrors." Even though Ma was just wheeled back from surgery and is barely coherent, she will fumble to answer a ringing telephone, knowing instinctively that it's one of her neglected offspring.

"There isn't anything to eat."

"I don't have any clean socks for school."

"Dad gave us Twinkies and Kool-Aid for breakfast."

"Where are the Band-Aids? The *big* Band-Aids?"

"Where is my blue sweater?"

Mother hangs up and worries. Will Kimberly and Ryan overdose on junk food? Who is bleeding? Will Bart the Bottomless Pit get so hungry that he eats that fossilized casserole in the refrigerator and has to have his stomach pumped?

How can parents handle these stresses? Obviously we are limited by our surroundings. We can't referee a fight between siblings or join in the search for a missing (and probably pregnant) hamster. We can't postpone an appendectomy until the kids are in college or married.

Until life returns to normal, we must cope with these major and minor upheavals the best way we can. Friends and extended family may be willing to supervise youngsters at home. We are not indispensable even though our young ones might try to convince us otherwise. We can only hope that some good will result from our absence. Perhaps this separation will help our children to become more self-reliant.

Also, let's try to keep things in perspective. Most of the chaotic events at home are not life-threatening and will be resolved without our intervention. May we be comforted in the knowledge that a diet of cookies and cola for a week rarely proves fatal.

But there *is* something we can do for our loved ones from our hospital bed. We can pray for them. Why not record special events involving our loved ones on a small calendar—"Kirk's baseball game," "Susie's test," or "Mary's school play." Then, on the appropriate day, we can remember them in our prayers. We feel close to our family as we ask God to bless their efforts to meet new challenges.

In addition to praying for our family, we can insist they stay home during some visiting hours. Spouses often become so fatigued from running to the hospital that they have to resist the urge to crawl into the nearest available bed.

To eliminate clutter from your mind, make a list of necessary errands and tasks: Return library books. Pick up the dry cleaning. And, if you don't want to stumble in your front door to be greeted by a morgue of brown foliage, add "water the plants." Also, why not have your mail brought to the hospital? You can easily sort through the six pounds of junk mail mixed in with the bills and ditch the trash immediately.

Delegate and explain responsibilities whenever possible. Obviously a teen-ager will be skilled in refrigerator usage, but may need detailed instructions about the use of the washing machine and dryer. Write out the directions from your bed and send them home to be posted above the appropriate appliance. (By the way, I hope you didn't leave your favorite sweater in the dirty clothes hamper. Your teen might "surprise" you and wash it in hot water along with the dirty towels! It will be clean, all right, but it won't fit anyone larger than a Cabbage Patch Doll.)

What other resources are available to draw upon? Don't be timid about asking people in your church for help. The body of Christ needs to learn how to give and receive support. Our own family has been blessed with a tremendous support network including extended family, church members, and friends. They have rallied to our need with delicious meals, housekeeping chores, transportation, and much more.

For those who ask, "Is there anything I can do?", go ahead and admit specific needs, then let the volunteer pick up on something he or she feels comfortable doing.

Finally, we patients must entrust our loved ones to the Lord's care. He loves them even more than we do. In Psalm 94:19, penned hundreds and thousands of years ago, we see that "cares of the heart" are nothing new. Anxiety plagued our ancestors too. When our cares are multiplied, how much more are we cheered by God's promises.

What does God promise? He promises to uphold and preserve the faithful (Ps. 31:23). "But from everlasting to everlasting the LORD's love is with those who fear him, and his righteousness with their children's children" (103:17).

How much does Jesus care for our little ones? When speaking of children in Matthew 18, Jesus said: "Their angels in heaven always see the face of my Father in heaven" (v. 10). What a comforting thought to a hospitalized parent fretting over children at home.

And God, who instituted the holy estate of marriage, cares equally for our partners. Surely we can safely entrust our little ones, our husbands, and our wives to his love and care. Like Laban, who faced separation from his beloved daughters and grandchildren, let us say: "The LORD keep watch between you and me when we are away from each other" (Gen. 31:49).

Lord, I've been so worried about everyone at home. When the phone rings I almost cringe, wondering what new crisis has erupted in my absence. My family misses me and needs me. I don't want to be away from them, but I know it is necessary. Help us all to trust you during this separation. Thank you, Lord. Amen.

TODAY I FELT SO HUMILIATED.

"I consider that our present sufferings are not worth comparing with the glory that will be revealed in us."

ROMANS 8:18

*B*y now you have learned the futility of trying to maintain any dignity while in the hospital. As a patient you may already have coped with bedpans, enemas, revealing gowns, and "The Public Bath." (For some reason physician visits and daily bathtime tend to coincide.) You might feel self-conscious when you must report urine output to a nurse of the opposite sex. And, of course, it's embarrassing when asked to peel off clothing for certain medical examinations and tests.

I've had my share of embarrassing moments too. Once, while hospitalized, I was attached to a catheter for several days. My minister popped in for a chat one evening. While we were visiting I happened to glance at the urine bag clipped to the bedframe. To my horror, it was leaking. I didn't want to draw attention to it by summoning a nurse. On the other hand, I would have been mortified if the plastic bag had ripped further, causing a flood in my corner of the room! I breathed a sigh of relief when my clergyman cut the visit short to check on another parishioner. Only then could I report the problem without risking further embarrassment.

Even a cardiac stress test can be humbling. As a patient I arrived at the appropriate testing area on a cart and stared curiously at the ominous equipment with its large screen and attached bike pedals. Finally my "big moment" came. I was assisted onto the seat and given the signal to begin pedaling. In less than two minutes the test was halted because of my racing heartbeat and breathing difficulties. "You can get off now and lie on the cart," instructed a tall, blond woman.

Nothing could have appealed to me more. However, neither leg would cooperate. There I sat, slumped over the machine, unable to dismount so that others could enjoy the "thrill of competition."

A cardiologist came to my rescue. "Would it be better if I were to lift you off?" I nodded gratefully and wrapped both arms around his neck. He placed my limp body on the cart.

I felt humiliated because I lacked muscle control, but the best was yet to come. A technician grumbled, "She's facing the wrong way."

Glancing down, I saw that the handle of the cart was at my feet. While that didn't strike me as being of tremendous importance, apparently it violated a strict code of patient transportation. Moving me became an issue.

Finally someone suggested, "Why not move the mattress around with her on it?" Four orderlies were pressed into service. Each clutched one side of the vinyl mattress and, on cue, heaved it (and me!) into the air. Then they paced a half-turn, stopped, and lowered the mattress. The technique worked, but I felt like a five-hundred-pound lady from a circus side show. Why did it take four men to move me? And without a safety net? If I am that heavy, I should wear a warning sign: "Extra-wide Load."

Other tests are equally degrading. Anyone who has endured a barium x-ray of the large intestine does not easily forget it. After barium is inserted, the patient is spun and tilted into ridiculous poses while the technician snaps candid shots. I doubt that even the most intrepid Hollywood stunt man would agree to be a "stand-in" for that caper.

Patients often feel that their bodies are on display. As if this were not humiliation enough, there are the insensitive comments of others to contend with.

Kathy, a friend, suffered deeply from the remarks of an attending physician. Kathy was extremely weak, but her scans and laboratory tests were negative. During visiting hours one afternoon the doctor barreled to her bedside and barked, "There is not a thing the matter with you! I want you to get up and go to that closet—which you are perfectly capable of doing—and get dressed. We need your bed for people who are *really sick!*" He turned on his heel and clicked out into the corridor.

Crushed, Kathy began to sob. Even her roommate was reduced to tears because of the doctor's cruelty. Stunned visitors who had been chatting with Kathy's roommate hastily made excuses to leave.

Months later Kathy learned that she had myasthenia gravis, a disorder that can result in death if not diagnosed in time. Kathy is grateful to be getting the proper treatment now, but this painful event still burns in her memory.

Rob, a thirty-five-year-old history teacher, having complained of double vision and difficulty in walking, experienced a similar trial at a midwest clinic. A team of neurologists ordered Rob to walk down the hospital corridor while they fanned out on either side to observe. Rob staggered and lost his balance repeatedly, weaving from side to side like a drunk.

To his dismay, the doctors taunted him: "Is that the best you can do, Rob?" "Oh come on now. You can walk better than *that!*" "You're just pretending. You can't fool us!"

Rob was devastated. He had never suffered such humiliation in his life. He figured he was crazy.

Even after a competent neurologist diagnosed Rob's problem—multiple sclerosis—this young man continued to doubt his own sanity. "Are you *sure* this isn't all in my head, Doctor?"

What is your source of humiliation? Are you incontinent? Did you have to wait too long for the bedpan? Did you feel robbed of your personhood during that test this morning? Perhaps someone made thoughtless remarks that wounded you.

Yes, you are hurting. You wonder how much more you can handle. You wish God would remove this cup of suffering forever. But whatever caused your embarrassment, you can receive abundant comfort from the Lord who truly understands.

Think of the degradation he endured. He was forced to disrobe—not for medical reasons—but before enemies who mocked him. Christ was scorned, spat upon, and arrayed in a purple robe. A crown of thorns was pressed into his tender flesh. His accusers jeered "Hail, King of the Jews" as they paraded our blessed Savior through crowded streets.

At Golgotha, Christ did not resist as his murderers nailed his hands and feet to a cross. As he hung, suspended in agony, soldiers cast lots for his seamless tunic. Throughout the crucifixion, the chief priests, elders, and scribes treated Jesus with contempt. One sneered, "He saved others, but he can't save himself" (Mark 15:31).

You and I cannot begin to imagine the depths of Jesus' physical and emotional suffering. He endured this deep humiliation for us and spilled his innocent blood so that we might have access to eternal life. Why? Only one reason. Because he loves us.

Our bodies are the temples of the Holy Spirit. As good stewards we have an obligation to take care of them. As a result, we may occasionally have to submit to embarrassing medical procedures. As we continue to grow older, we may feel cheated when bodily functions fail. Sometimes we may have to depend on transfusions, pacemakers, insulin, donor organs, or an assortment of plastic and mechanical replacement parts. We may even feel that we are being recycled!

Our suffering isn't pleasant, but it doesn't weigh much on God's balance scales. The apostle Paul knew.

"I consider that our present sufferings are not worth comparing with the glory that will be revealed in us" (Rom. 8:18).

Is God denying that we feel pain? Not at all. Our heavenly Father is aware of the intensity of our suffering, our humiliation, our embarrassment. But he also has intimate knowledge of what lies in store for believers. He guarantees that these temporary trials can't compare with the everlasting joy that is to be ours. We will receive a glorified body. The Lord Jesus Christ will come for us as a trumpet sounds. We will pass victoriously through the portals of heaven and into fellowship with him forever.

Embarrassed? Of course you are. Remember, though, this affliction is but for a moment. Look beyond this trial to the glory that will be revealed.

Father, I felt violated today. I'm worn-out from the tests. I'm tired of people probing and poking at my body as if I'm some science specimen. But my humiliation seems small and insignificant when I remember how Jesus suffered at the hands of his enemies—for me! I'm so unworthy, but the Son of God died for me under the most embarrassing of circumstances. What love! In Christ's name. Amen.

I'VE NEVER BEEN THIS WEAK BEFORE.

"My grace is sufficient for you, for my power is made perfect in weakness."

2 CORINTHIANS 12:9

*E*velyn was so weak when her husband rushed her to the emergency room one terrifying evening that she could easily have died. She couldn't walk, stand, or hold up her head. Months later, Evelyn learned that she had a neuromuscular disease. Victims of this disease often experience temporary "paralysis" of some or all of their muscles. Breathing and heart rate may be affected. A few patients die in crisis when medication is unbalanced. Simple acts like bathing, shampooing, talking, or writing may be difficult or even impossible to accomplish when the patient is fatigued.

Such a handicap causes upheaval in life, altering goals and expectations. At times Evelyn has to depend on a cane or wheelchair because her leg muscles tire so easily. Though she doesn't welcome reduced stamina, she is learning to accept this illness and its limitations.

Are you weak from surgery or sickness? Are you

immobile due to paralysis? My heart goes out to you as I, too, continue to cope with weakness. Those of us who struggle with this problem may feel trapped in our own bodies. Even though young in years, we may feel older than the century. No one enjoys the restrictions that such weakness imposes on our lifestyles. How comforting, though, that we can turn to God for hope and help.

The apostle Paul wrestled with a physical impairment. While the Scriptures never specifically identify Paul's malady, obviously he found it a hindrance. He regarded it so disruptive to his ministry that he beseeched God three times to deliver him from this "thorn in the flesh." What was God's response? The Lord assured Paul, "My grace is sufficient for you, for my power is made perfect in weakness" (2 Cor. 12:9).

Did Paul grumble and denounce God? Not to our knowledge. He accepted God's final decision even though it was hardly the answer he had hoped for. Paul went on to exclaim that in the future he would *brag* about his weakness so that Christ's power would rest on him. He concluded, "For when I am weak, then I am strong" (2 Cor. 12:10).

Is that some kind of pious double talk? Not really. Paul understood that the heavenly Father was promising him an increase in spiritual strength. How did Paul receive this offer? By acknowledging and accepting his own weakness. Then, and only then, could Paul's empty vessel become filled with God's unlimited strength.

Today much emphasis is placed on physical fitness. Many people jog, swim, walk briskly, or dance in aerobics classes. Others work out at health and fitness centers. You and I may never be able to obtain to the Presidential Award for Physical Fitness, since most of us would be overjoyed just to be able to carry out normal activities again.

Even though physically frail, we have the potential to become stronger than we ever thought possible. Ironic, isn't it? We may be pitiful specimens of physical fitness, but God can transform us into models of spiritual strength.

As we reflect on this thought, let's examine another biblical passage. In his first letter to Timothy, Paul wrote, "Train yourself to be godly. For physical training is of some value, but godliness has value for all things, holding promise for both the present life and the life to come" (4:7–8).

What is the message? Physical fitness has temporary benefits, but developing godliness will pay off both in this life and for all eternity as we learn how to live and love as children of God. The Bible strengthens the inner person with the abundant riches of God's grace.

We grow by feeding on God's Word, devouring the Scriptures faithfully. We are told, "Let the word of Christ dwell in you richly" (Col. 3:16). Can we "flesh out" spiritually if we only occasionally snack on biblical truths? Certainly not. No more than an athlete can succeed if he devotes only one day per week to training. For optimum results our spiritual training program must occur on a daily basis as well. The key word in this Scripture verse is *richly*. As we invest plenty of time in Bible study we are able to digest the "meat" of the Scriptures, thereby developing spiritual biceps.

What results from scriptural training? We become well-equipped and thoroughly instructed as disciples of Christ. With or without the actual use of our legs, we learn to "walk by the Spirit," resisting sinful, fleshly desires. Our ultimate aim? "To live a life worthy of the Lord." As we make it our goal to please him, we will be "bearing fruit in every good work, growing in the knowledge of God" (Col. 1:10). As we grow and change, fruits of the Spirit—love, joy, peace, patience, kindness, goodness, faithfulness, gentleness, and self-control—become evident.

Because of physical impairments, various obstacles may block your path. For example, some patients are too weak to support a Bible. If you are one of them, perhaps you can manage to turn pages independently if the Bible is balanced on a lap tray. Clipboards hold devotional material adequately and provide a convenient writing surface. The visually handicapped and patients unable to use their arms benefit from a variety of Christian tapes. Why not ask your church to provide volunteer readers? Assess the problem and seek a workable solution.

Despite infirmities and related hurdles, we reach for an attainable goal. We can be nourished by God's Word even though we are physically unable to feed ourselves from that lunch tray. Each day we can stretch, bend, grow, and achieve new heights in a spiritual sense. And when our life ends, we can look forward to eternal bliss in the presence of Christ Jesus. These broken bodies will be transformed into whole, healed, perfect bodies that will surpass all our hopes.

Let's say with Paul, "I press on toward the goal to win the prize for which God has called me heavenward in Christ Jesus" (Phil. 3:14). In spite of our feeble bodies, our heavenly Father can use us in beautiful ways to further the kingdom of God on earth. The Holy Spirit empowers us to adore Christ even during painful trials. When others witness our unwavering faith and attitude of praise during tribulation, they are edified. Our example inspires them to trust God for the outcome when they wrestle with adversity.

Christians, sick or well, face challenges. We struggle against sin and despair as we endeavor to lead a sanctified life. The writer of Hebrews called this battle a "race." His advice for participants was as follows: "Let us throw off everything that hinders and the sin that so easily entangles, and let us run with perseverance the race marked out for us. Let us fix our eyes on Jesus, the author and perfecter of our faith, who for the joy set before him endured the cross, scorning its shame, and sat down at the right hand of the throne of God" (Heb. 12:1–2).

You and I are currently "in training." We are blessed with a Divine Coach who sponsors a winning team. Our heavenly victory is guaranteed. When the Son of Man appears in glory to claim his own, we will say, "I have fought the good fight, I have finished the race, I have kept the faith" (2 Tim. 4:7).

Dear Father, it's exciting to realize that the power of God is available to me. That knowledge makes this present weakness bearable. Oh, sometimes I'm afraid. I wonder how much weaker I'll get and if I'll ever be normal again. Help me to put these worries aside and concentrate on gaining spiritual strength. Enable me to finish the race! In Jesus' name. Amen.

I FEEL LIKE A BURDEN.

"Hear my cry, O God; listen to my prayer.
From the ends of the earth I call to you, I
call as my heart grows faint."

PSALM 61:1–2

*C*ertain aspects of a hospital stay are endurable, if not actually enjoyable. Patients initially respond favorably to all the attention. They unwrap gifts, nibble chocolates, and proudly display flowers, plants, and get-well cards. This enthusiasm soon fades, and by the second day, it's downhill all the way. As the flowers wilt, so does the patient. He or she becomes grouchy and begins the countdown until it is time to go home.

As the stay stretches on, threatening to surpass the length of the Korean War, another problem may surface. Long, drawn-out illnesses cause some patients to feel like burdens. Self-esteem begins to crumble. A few become so saturated with feelings of worthlessness that they become bitter.

Consider Carl's situation. This successful businessman was rushed to a cardiac care unit with a dangerous heart condition. As days melted into weeks, Carl became a kaleidoscope of feelings. He was angry at the "unfairness" of it all and frightened by the future. Worst of all, he felt like a burden to his wife and children. Never in his thirty-eight years had he been sick. He had always taken charge of his family and made the decisions.

Now the situation was reversed. Martha and the kids hovered over him like he was an invalid. No one consulted him. Carl felt worthless. His despondency increased to the point that he considered suicide. He thought, *If I kill myself, I'll be out of their way once and for all.* A psychiatrist intervened before Carl could carry out his warped plan.

Like Carl, I struggled with bouts of self-pity. When I was healthy, I took pride in my independence and ability to "produce." When illness prevented me from carrying out my normal roles as wife, mother, and teacher, I was frustrated, angry, and guilt-stricken. I hated to see my husband, John, assuming my responsibilities. He didn't complain, but I considered myself an albatross around his neck. My self-esteem plummeted.

I remember my husband's shock when I blurted out one evening, "It would have been better if I had died!" I foolishly believed my death would spell his freedom.

My mate began the long process of assuring me that I am needed, not because of what I can accomplish, but because I am Gloria. In time, I believed him.

My daily Bible studies were helpful as well. I frequently read the book of Philippians and marveled at Paul's joy and peace of mind during his imprisonment.

My problems seemed small by comparison. Eventually I could claim with Paul, "Yes, and I will continue to rejoice, for I know that through your prayers and the help given by the Spirit of Jesus Christ, what has happened to me will turn out for my deliverance" (Phil. 1:18–19).

Today I no longer measure my self-worth in terms of homemade cookies, freshly baked bread, handsewn garments, or volunteer efforts. It's a good thing! Most of these activities are "off limits" because of my physical restrictions.

What about you? Are you battling feelings of inferiority? Do you ever lash out at your caretakers? Have you ever thought that your loved ones would be better off if you were out of the picture?

Chase those thoughts from your head with a vengeance. Now! A low self-image does not enhance one's personality. Negative feelings spill over like acid, damaging relationships and eating away at your insides. You will generate about as much "fun" as a poison adder at a tea party. In other words, folks will find plenty of reasons for avoiding you.

Naturally, you are concerned about the effects your illness is having on your family. They look shell-shocked. Their social life consists of shuttling back and forth to the hospital, washing your pajamas, paying the bills, and covering for you at home. You may think, *Yeah, I know. And it's all my fault.*

Is it really your fault that you are sick? Did you, one bright sunny day decide, "Life is rather dull. I think I'll develop some kidney stones to stir up a little action. And let's see how an inflamed appendix could complicate the plot!" Of course not! These circumstances were beyond your control.

Now that you have been pronounced "Innocent of Health Crimes," why not work to eliminate those feelings of inferiority? The Lord will help. You can pray King David's prayer: "Hear my cry, O God; listen to my prayer. From the ends of the earth I call to you, I call as my heart grows faint" (Ps. 61:1–2).

Isn't that appropriate? By now you probably figure that your hospital bed might as well be at the ends of the earth. No matter where you are, God hears your plea just as he heard my cry and Carl's. Although Carl's heart was weakened by disease, he suffered primarily from emotional pain, a "faint heart." You and I often succumb to the "faint heart syndrome" too, don't we?

Let's talk about the basis of self-worth. Are we valuable for our productivity? Unfortunately, the world transmits this very message and we buy it. We are impressed by resumés, credentials, college degrees, book credits, and medals. In the spirit of competition, we may strive to be on the dean's list. We secretly aspire to be Salesperson of the Year, Outstanding Teacher, Neighbor of the Month, or author of a best-seller.

Now, it's fine to earn these awards. However, our self-worth shouldn't depend on them. We are just as valuable with or without our labels, certificates, trophies, pedigrees, and bronzed plaques.

Ask yourself honestly: Am I living to please

others and receive their praise, or to please God and give him the glory? Scripture tells us, "Whatever you do, do it all for the glory of God" (1 Cor. 10:31). God's approval is the ultimate test.

Does the Lord keep accounts entitled "Outstanding Christians of the Century" or "Top Ten Believers"? Not at all. Oh, as I've mentioned before, he does keep a book—the Book of Life. It contains the names of the redeemed who trust in Christ. That saving faith is what determines our admittance into heaven, not our achievements in PTA, the United Fund Drive, or the annual church bazaar.

God is aware of our motives, isn't he? Nothing is hidden from our heavenly Father. "The LORD does not look at the things man looks at. Man looks at the outward appearance, but the LORD looks at the heart" (1 Sam. 16:7).

The apostle Paul had his priorities straight. At Philippi, he reminded the believers: "Put no confidence in the flesh" (3:3). Then Paul elaborated on his "credentials," explaining that he was circumcised, brought up as a Hebrew, and considered zealous and blameless under the Law. Finally he made the most important statement of all: "But whatever was to my profit I now consider loss for the sake of Christ. What is more, I consider everything a loss compared to the surpassing greatness of knowing Christ Jesus my Lord, for whose sake I have lost all things. I consider them rubbish, that I may gain Christ" (vv. 7–8). Paul knew that the knowledge of salvation is far more precious than any earthly possession or achievement. All else—

our awards, medals, and laurels—stack up as "rubbish" by comparison.

We might ask, "Do we count? Are we important? If our value isn't determined by what we do, then how can we be worth anything to the Lord?" He loves us because of who we are. We are his creation, fashioned by his hands and filled with the breath of life. "God saw all that he had made, and it was very good" (Gen. 1:31) Even when sin entered the world, God's plan for open communication with his creatures was not thwarted. "For God so loved the world that he gave his one and only Son, that whoever believes in him shall not perish but have eternal life" (John 3:16) The justice of God (demanding a penalty for sin) joined the unconditional love of God and nailed our sins to the cross of Jesus Christ, the only perfect man who ever lived.

You and I are so important that the Creator of the Universe redeemed us with the blood of his "one and only" Son. Through Jesus, we belong to a royal bloodline. As sons and daughters of the King we will dwell in a heavenly palace.

As a child of God, you belong to the body of Christ, which carries out his work on earth. Why not allow others the pleasure of serving you? If the situation were reversed, wouldn't you gladly do the same for them? Well, then, swallow that pride and accept the love and support that others ache to give you. In turn, serve them by your prayers and expressions of appreciation. Offer a listening ear, give encouragement, and make their visits pleasant by your Christ-like attitude.

We are not burdens, after all. Even though sick,

we can be servants of Christ and of one another. Let's respond to that challenge with love.

Lord, I have been guilty of thinking that I am self-sufficient. Well, I'm not. I find that I need others more than ever before. Most of all, I need you, Father. Help me to view this "confession" as a sign of growth. Thank you, Lord, for creating, redeeming, and loving me. Enable me to love and accept myself. In Jesus' name. Amen.

I THINK GOD HAS
ABANDONED ME.

"Why, O LORD, do you stand far off? Why
do you hide yourself in times of trouble?"

PSALM 10:1

*H*ave you lost all hope? Does it feel as if you're
making an endurance run and can't hold out to
cross the finish line? If so, Psalm 22 might sum up your
emotions at this time. It is a messianic Psalm, the words
of which were spoken by Christ on the cross. In agony
he cried, "Eli, Eli, lama sabachthani!"

In English, the words mean, "My God, my God,
why have you forsaken me?" From this verse alone, we
can assume that Jesus endured emotional pain as well
as extreme physical suffering. Wasn't he, in effect,
asking, "Where are you, Father? I feel alone, forgotten,
and separated from you." Think of it. Even the Messiah
felt abandoned by God for a time.

Psalm 22 has a lot more to say about pain and
suffering and hopelessness: "Why are you so far from
saving me, so far from the words of my groaning? O my

God, I cry out by day, but you do not answer; by night, and am not silent."

Perhaps this particular verse speaks to you. When heartaches multiply you may feel that God is far away. You may even begin to doubt that he can hear your prayers for help. You feel so alone. Forsaken. Forgotten.

Marcy Anderson's incredible trials caused her to question her faith. Her physical health mysteriously nosedived. Robbed of stamina, she had to quit her job as a pediatric nurse. Tests eventually showed that Marcy has a rare incurable illness. Her doctor emphasized the importance of rest, good nutrition, and avoidance of unnecessary stress. Unfortunately, Marcy's husband, Craig, didn't believe the diagnosis. He refused to discuss her disease and failed to support her. When he saw her lying on the couch, he was angry.

Marcy says, "He never acknowledged that I was sick. Since I looked fine, he expected me to 'perform' as usual. At first I catered to his demands. Sometimes when I fixed supper, though, I was so exhausted I cried."

In the meantime, Craig Anderson was wallowing in self-pity. It wasn't fair that his wife claimed to be sick. It wasn't his fault. Besides, he didn't understand how anyone who looked so healthy could really be sick. He spent less and less time with Marcy, turning his attentions to a young secretary in his law office. An affair followed, and Craig eventually sued his wife for divorce.

"When the court summons arrived, I was shocked," admits Marcy. "I had already lost my job and my health. Now it appeared that I was going to lose my husband too! Not that our marriage was perfect. Still, I needed some stability in my life."

Marcy, a Christian, prayed that God would forgive her for what she was about to do. One October night she climbed into their blue sedan and careened down the highway. As she inched the accelerator closer and closer to the floorboard, she wailed, "God, where are you? Don't you care?"

Suddenly she thought of her red-headed daughter, Megan. If she killed herself, her little girl wouldn't have a mother. Marcy reduced her speed to normal. She prayed, reciting the Twenty-third Psalm over and over again. A sense of peace replaced her fear. With God's help, she would endure. She had to. Megan needed her. Drained but determined, Marcy drove home.

The next months were not easy, but Marcy survived. She drew on God's never-ending source of strength. In time she felt well enough to resume working on a part-time basis. And, at church, she met a compassionate widower who understands her limitations and is fond of Megan. The future looks bright for this divorcée.

What burdens are you shouldering? Are you frustrated because you feel that God isn't hearing or responding to your prayers? Are you envious of others who seem to breeze through life, plagued with fewer problems? Like the psalmist you might moan, "Why, O

Lord, do you stand far off? Why do you hide yourself in times of trouble?" (Ps. 10:1).

On the cross, Jesus felt momentarily abandoned, but God had not forgotten about his only Son. Jesus' suffering was part of the plan—to accomplish our salvation by paying the penalty for our sins. And on the third day a miraculous event occurred—Jesus rose from the dead! A grave couldn't contain God's Son. Through his spilled blood we have access to the Father and can confidently pray, "Answer me when I call to you, O my righteous God" (Ps. 4:1).

The Lord has not really turned his face from you. This earthly body—this house encasing the spirit—is constantly bombarded by trials and tribulations. When trouble weighs you down, you may feel as desperate as Marcy who wasn't afraid to die—but was afraid to live! The future appeared black and grim, and she felt as if she were stumbling about in the dark without direction.

How did she cope? By leaning on God and trusting him. In her Bible she underlined Psalm 119:105: "Your word is a lamp to my feet and a light for my path." God's Word was Marcy's light, illuminating her path just enough that she could "see herself through" one day at a time. The Father equipped her to handle chronic illness and a shattered marriage. Had she been granted a peek at tomorrow, Marcy would have been surprised to see blessings ahead.

God never abandons us even though we may sometimes feel forgotten. Despite our feelings, his promises remain true. In Scripture we read, "For I am convinced that neither death nor life, neither angels nor demons, neither the present nor the future, nor any powers, neither height nor depth, nor anything else in all creation, will be able to separate us from the love of God that is in Christ Jesus our Lord" (Rom. 8:38).

What a comfort. Even though your particular situation may seem intolerable, God is with you. Already he is working on a plan of escape for you. You will pass safely through this crisis. Furthermore, God has promised you an abundance of spiritual blessings. Above this present darkness shines a dazzling light. A glorious day awaits the believer in Christ.

O Lord, I have questioned my faith and doubted your existence. I'm so overwhelmed by this health crisis that my most precious beliefs are shaken. Please forgive me. My path looks dark and frightening. Reassure me that I am not alone. May your Word be my lifeline and my hope. In Jesus' name. Amen.

AT NIGHT I CAN'T STOP CRYING.

"Record my lament; list my tears on your scroll—are they not in your record?"

PSALM 56:8

*E*ven the most stoic individual may often be on the verge of tears while hospitalized. In some health institutions the food alone is enough to make one weep. After all, who enjoys eating mashed potatoes that taste like a mixture of school paste and papier-mâché?

Yet that's only one reason why patients lack patience and resort to tears. Depressing physical surroundings, unpleasant odors, communication problems, conflicts with hospital personnel or roommates—all these only compound the problem when a person is already anxious about test results and probable surgeries.

For starters, let's consider how the environment can negatively affect one's moods. Allow me to insert a personal experience that took place when I was admitted to a sprawling medical center several miles from our home.

After I had signed in, a volunteer rolled my wheelchair over frayed orange carpeting as we threaded our way through dark, musty corridors. My husband trailed behind, toting my suitcase. At journey's end the cheerful matron deposited me in a four-bed ward. "Well," she chirped. "This is it."

I gripped the arms of my wheelchair, too shocked to speak. This dismal room looked like it hadn't been redecorated since the Truman administration. Faded, gray tweed wallpaper hung in shreds. Bare pipes crisscrossed the high ceiling. Roach motels populated the floor and yellowed privacy curtains were punctured with rips and tears. The four narrow beds were jammed so close together that we patients could have timed each other's respiration rates.

I found my voice and addressed an aide scurrying toward me with a package. "Do I *have* to stay here?" I whispered.

She stiffened. "Everyone always gripes when they see this ward! Do you realize that there is a waiting list a mile long for this hospital?" She flung a bundle of supplies on my broken nightstand. "You were lucky to get a room at all!" With her head held high, Miss Congeniality stomped out the door.

Properly humbled, I sat on the lumpy mattress and fought tears. Somehow I didn't feel lucky. This miserable ward resembled a slum tenement.

My mate looked at me with pity in his eyes. "This is, well, just unbelievable!"

"Do you suppose prison cells are this bad?"

"I doubt it. There are laws, you know. But you

won't be here long," he reminded me. "You can handle it for a few days, can't you?"

I gritted my teeth. "I'll try," I promised. I had one flicker of hope. Maybe my room would be condemned and I'd get an early release.

As I settled in to be a "regular" in that miserable place, I studied the reactions of new patients as they took up residence in the room. Some embraced their stomachs and laughed uproariously when they first saw it. Most, though, reacted as I had—with tears.

Communication problems may also cause stress. Some physicians won't talk. In contrast, some bunkmates won't *stop* talking! (We've already discussed that little bonus problem.)

Traumatic events erupting around you can also frazzle your nerves. You hear a rumor that a young person on your floor has died. When sirens wail or someone screams in pain, you flinch. Your roommate may be scheduled for a spinal tap and you're afraid you're going to be an unwilling witness. A code blue alert is sounded. Your heart skips a beat as you hear doctors and nurses thundering down the corridor in a frantic attempt to save a life.

Patients have ample reason to cry. Those too embarrassed to weep in public hold back their tears until dark, when the privacy curtain is drawn and lights are dimmed. Then worries, like phantoms, flit in and out of the mind to taunt and haunt.

Whenever you weep, remember that your crying is beneficial. Tears reduce stress and release pent-up emotions. God made us to feel, so we need not be ashamed of our humanness. Jesus understands. After all, when his friends Mary and Martha were mourning their beloved brother, Jesus wept too. He felt sorrow even though he knew that it would all come out right in the end—that he planned to miraculously restore Lazarus's life. Mourners soon witnessed that unforgettable event.

Why are you crying? Are you fearful of the unknown? Is your life on earth drawing to a close? Will you leave little ones behind? Why do you toss and turn during the night?

God has kept a record of your sleepless nights. Isn't that remarkable? The Lord of the Universe knows when you are restless. Your troubled thoughts are not a surprise to him. He cares. King David, full of sorrow, made a request of the Lord: "Record my lament." God stores up each one of your tears as well.

When you can't sleep, visualize Jesus sitting in that chair next to your bed. You can safely close your eyes, because he never takes his eyes off you. He wants you to rest. "He grants sleep to those he loves" (Ps. 127:2).

And there is more! The Scriptures promise: "Weeping may remain for a night, but rejoicing comes in the morning" (Ps. 30:5). Your particular "night" may seem to be lasting an eternity. It seems so long since you felt the warmth of sunshine or saw a glimpse of daylight because of this affliction. Even so, God is with you. He hugs you to his heart even tighter during the blackest hour of a crisis.

When we enter the glorious gates of the New Jerusalem, we will not sorrow any more. We are told, "On no day will its gates ever be shut, for there will be no night there" (Rev. 21:25). Nor will sunlight and moonlight be necessary because "The glory of God gives it light, and the Lamb is its lamp" (v. 23).

And what about our tears? They will have ceased. "[God] will wipe every tear from their eyes. There will be no more death or mourning or crying or pain, for the old order of things has passed away" (Rev. 21:4).

What marvelous promises! Never again will we have reason to weep. Perfect joy will be ours at last.

Dear Father, I've been a bundle of raw emotions. Half the time I don't understand why I'm crying. I'm embarrassed when others catch me, though it comforts me to remember that Mary and Martha saw the Son of God shedding tears. None of my tears escapes his notice. How wonderful that the Lord of the Universe pays such close attention. Thank you, Father, for the glorious morning that is coming. In Jesus' name. Amen.

THE DOCTORS DON'T KNOW WHAT'S WRONG WITH ME.

"Hope in God, for I will yet praise him."
PSALM 43:5

*L*uke, a husky auto mechanic, began to experience bizarre symptoms. His muscles twitched violently and he stumbled often. Luke, skilled in auto repair, expected his physician to correct these physical problems with equal success. Many visits to the doctor, hospitalizations, and fees later, Luke still copes with the unknown. Doctors agree that something is wrong, but no one can pinpoint the cause. Because of increasing fatigue, Luke has had to quit his job. He is angry, confused, and afraid.

Most people expect instant diagnoses, but elusive illnesses are difficult to isolate. It takes time and perseverance on behalf of both physician and patient. Many patients are observed for weeks, months, or even years before the sickness is properly tagged with a name.

Most victims of neuromuscular illnesses and rare diseases undergo severe emotional and physical trials before eventual diagnosis. Many have unnecessary surgeries. Some are incorrectly labeled mentally ill, one common misdiagnosis being conversion reaction. Upon referral to a psychiatrist, the patient may then be told that no emotional problem exists. So another physician is consulted and the cycle repeats itself. Juggled between mental health professionals and doctors with no firm answers, many people become so discouraged that emotional problems do develop.

Does this sound heartbreakingly familiar? Are you questioning your own sanity because of a similar crisis? You aren't alone. Thousands, perhaps more, walk this tightrope.

Allow me to share my painful ordeal with the unknown factor in illness. I ignored the early warning signals. For example, I had difficulty driving our VW but assumed the car needed fixing, not the driver— even when I couldn't keep the brake pedal depressed at stoplights and found the steering wheel "too hard" to turn. It never occurred to me that something was wrong with my body.

More symptoms appeared as the months continued. My hands fatigued rapidly when I played the piano and my vision blurred. Climbing a flight of steps left me limp and exhausted, as if I'd trekked to the top of the Washington Monument. A bout with the "flu" resulted in more deterioration. I could no longer hold myself erect long enough to eat. Muscles didn't respond to messages from the brain, but the problem couldn't be detected in my appearance. The only changes were sagging facial muscles and "droopy" eyes. My children would ask, "Mom, are you mad?"

I finally sought help. Physicians first labeled my problem a strain of flu, strep infection, viral infection, or possibly rheumatic fever, then changed their minds and opted for something more exotic: anemia, bone marrow irregularity, mild diabetes. I felt as if I were a charter member of the "Disease of the Month Club." A team of specialists ordered dozens of tests and scans. I regarded these physicians as a squad of detectives engrossed in a game of "Medical Clue."

It was no fun. Desperate for answers, I began to question my mental status. Folks encouraged me, "We are praying for your tests to be normal." I appreciated the prayers, but knew normal results only meant more tests. "Medical Clue" would drag on until the answer surfaced.

During visiting hours a retired pastor dropped by my hospital room for a chat. "How is it going? Do you know anything yet?"

I managed a weak smile. "Yes, I now know of 1,234 diseases that I *don't* have."

He probed beneath the surface humor. "So, they still don't know what's wrong with you, do they?"

I shook my head. "There's still one more test. It might give me the answer.

"Listen to me, Gloria. Your hope is in God. Your hope doesn't rest in these doctors or tests. Trust God in this."

Exactly! I had trusted in God for salvation, but I was trusting in Doctors A, B, and C for the answers to my weakness. I had not totally surrendered this sickness to the Lord. That complete yielding came months later when I returned from a clinic. The attending physician had treated me as if I were a hypochondriac and hadn't even bothered to unseal all my medical reports.

At first I simply wanted to die. I saw no hope for the future. *Lord,* I prayed, *I can't go on. I give up.* But God held me firmly throughout that bleak period of despair and assured me through his Word that he had not abandoned me. I surrendered my body and my future to his care. Psalm 43:5 sums up my feelings. "Hope in God, for I will yet praise him, my Savior and my God."

Within weeks tests showed I had myasthenia gravis, a condition that responds to medication. However, an additional problem illness causes me to "lose" patterns of walking and results in scrambled, weakened messages from the brain. The full answer has not yet been revealed.

Can I continue to live in the realm of the unknown? Yes, with God's help, though I prefer answers. Preferably *today.* It's easier to cope with the known factors in life. However, I cannot alter my circumstances. God has enabled me to come this far without "breaking" and he'll provide strength for tomorrow.

If you face a similar problem, insist that extensive testing be done. In certain situations it is advisable to consult another physician. Another doctor might have a more thorough approach and be able to fit the puzzle pieces together. In many instances, though, patients have to accept the fact that no answers are currently available.

Beth, a friend, has battled an unidentified neuro-muscular illness for six years. She finds it challenging to keep up with five lively youngsters when she is constantly exhausted. More frustrating than the deep fatigue, though, is the mental anguish. Naturally, Beth asks herself, "What is this? Will it get worse? Would medication help? Is surgery dangerous when I am so weak?"

Not long ago she confessed to her physician, "Listen, I don't mind 'taking the trip.' Whatever disease I have, I'll handle it. But, please give me the road map. I'll face the detours when I get there."

Dr. Henderson shook his head. He aches to give Beth the road map, but it isn't possible right now. Beth must continue living with the uncertainties that cloud her future.

Has your doctor thrown up his hands? "I'm sorry. I really don't know what's wrong." Have you been told that there is nothing medical science can do to help you and that you must learn to accept the situation as it is?

This is a tough struggle, isn't it? You have no idea which, if any, drugs might help. You can't rush off to a support group meeting because you don't know which one you should join, though you long for emotional support. You can't even read a library book about an illness that has no name.

Has life ended? No. When human resources fail, there is only one place left to go—to the Creator who knows every cell and molecule in your body. The almighty Father will teach you to trust him more.

Someone does have a complete "road map" of your life, which includes details of your illness. The Lord holds this knowledge.

In the days and months ahead, you may journey through unknown territory. In the rough, slippery places you may tremble for fear that you will slip into the abyss. Don't be afraid. You are not traveling alone. The Good Shepherd walks beside you. There is no unfamiliar territory to him. He will guide you through these fiery trials, one by one. And you will emerge from affliction, unharmed.

Dear Father, how long must I continue to cope with the unknown? Some days I don't think I can endure this uncertainty any longer. Lord, you hold the answer to all mysteries. If it is your will, lead me to the proper diagnosis. Above all, increase my patience and enable me to trust you with the question marks of my future. In Jesus' name. Amen.

NO ONE UNDERSTANDS HOW I REALLY FEEL.

"My soul is in anguish."

PSALM 6:3

J anet, a former nurse, is afflicted with a neuro-muscular illness. When she gets tired she experiences a deep fatigue that a normal person cannot begin to comprehend. After too much activity her muscles simply refuse to work for a time.

While hospitalized, Janet became exhausted from the extensive testing procedures. Limp as a rag doll, she lay flat on her bed, too weak even to hold a book.

During evening visiting hours a neighbor arrived, clutching a stack of magazines and a bouquet of yellow daisies. Margo smiled. "How are you doing today?"

Janet hesitated. "To tell you the truth, I'm wiped out from all those tests."

Margo deposited her gifts on the nightstand and perched on the end of a hard, wooden chair. "I know just how you feel. Why today I played golf, went out to lunch, fixed supper, and did three loads of wash. I thought I'd die!"

Hurt was reflected in Janet's eyes. *She doesn't understand at all,* she thought. *I can't even walk around a golf course on my good days. I'd be happy if I could just sit in that chair. I wish. . . ."*

Janet didn't risk verbalizing her thoughts. She didn't want to offend Margo. Besides, Margo might think she was a hypochrondriac.

Like Janet, I have a physical disability that cannot be seen. I, too, have often felt misunderstood. For example, I recall lying in a hospital bed, almost paralyzed, a few years ago. Doctors hadn't yet diagnosed my illness, and I was scared. One afternoon two acquaintances bustled to my bedside. Helen peered at me through her bifocals. "My, you look marvelous!" she exclaimed heartily, then turned to her younger friend. "Doesn't she look great, Sue?"

Sue agreed. "Oh, yes. She looks so healthy."

At a loss for an answer, I swallowed hard. How could I expect these ladies to believe that I lacked the strength to support my own head? Would they care to listen while I shared my horror at not being able to raise my arms above my shoulders for an x-ray?

I kept those chilling thoughts to myself and focused on my visitors. We chatted about the weather, our kids, and the sale at Baldwin's Department Store.

I kept up the pretense and was quick with witticisms. It was easier to chat about a thunderstorm and a clearance sale than to admit my fears. Facing reality would have been too painful, so I conveniently hid behind a mask. This mask kept others from discerning my true feelings. I couldn't chance being misunderstood or pitied. Denial became my favorite defense mechanism.

Does this sound familiar? Do you sometimes bury your feelings and ramble on about everything but what concerns you the most right now? On the other hand, you may not deny your illness at all. You may have attempted to unload on your friends and family. You still shudder at their responses.

Your best friend acted tense and actually changed the subject when you spoke of your possible cancer. Your spouse forced a smile and said, "Don't worry about it" when you wanted to discuss the effect your illness might have on your children and your career. When you hinted that you might die, your sister looked horrified and scolded, "Don't even talk like that!"

Are others sidestepping your questions and concerns? You may be willing to "tell all," but that is no guarantee that your loved ones can handle it. They are hurting too and may be so overwhelmed that they are incapable of ministering to your needs. You feel like someone is trying to put a cork on your negative emotions.

Perhaps you did bare your soul to a friend. Afterward, the person announced, as Margo did to Janet, "I know just how you feel." Your friend meant well, of course, but such a comment offered little comfort. Does this healthy person know what it is like to face disfiguring surgery? Has this individual wrestled with an unknown factor in illness?

Your situation may be further complicated by traumatic events such as a divorce, the death of a loved one, a major move, or a job change. You may be so devastated by other recent stresses in your life that this crisis ranks low on your list of worries. You feel so alone.

Thanks be to God, you are not really alone. There is One and only One who knows how you feel. Just think how often Jesus was misunderstood during his earthly ministry. When he attempted to explain his approaching death and resurrection to his disciples, they missed the point entirely. Later, when they accompanied Christ to the Garden of Gethsemane, they were instructed to "watch and pray." Our Lord prayed in great agony of soul. And the disciples? They fell asleep!

God is well-acquainted with your sickness, fear, and the upheavals in your life. He is by your side, offering his strength for this trial.

Scripture reminds us in Psalm 34:18, "The LORD is close to the brokenhearted." Picture his loving arms stretching out to receive you as a father soothes a troubled child. To return the embrace, you must drop this weight of worry. Just let it go.

You are free. God has forgiven your sins through Christ and wants you to have peace. God will take over now and carry your burdens for you. He'll even carry *you* when necessary. It's a promise. Psalm 55:22 says, "Cast your cares on the LORD and he will sustain you."

Father, I've been so frustrated today. Sometimes I felt as if I were going to explode. Please grant me courage to face my fears and deal with my feelings. Help me to be patient with friends and family who are trying to support me. Thank you, Lord, that your support never wavers. You are always available to listen, understand, and guide. All praise to you, Father. In Jesus' name. Amen.

WHY WON'T GOD HEAL ME?

"Commit your way to the LORD; trust in
him and he will do this."

PSALM 37:5

*F*or eight years many Christians have faithfully
prayed for my healing. Nevertheless, I remain
ill. Does the Almighty have it "in" for me? Do I doubt
God's power to heal? Is my faith too weak?

I've been approached by people who suggest my
faith is inadequate. One of these encounters took place
in a hospital. Karen, a hospital employee, waltzed into
my room and pulled up a chair. "I've been wanting to
talk to you. I understand you are a believer."

"Yes, I am."

Karen got to the point. "Well, since the doctors
haven't diagnosed you yet, don't you suppose this
illness is from Satan?"

I bristled. "Satan?"

"Yes, Satan. He wants you so you can't serve the
Lord. Right now, you aren't of any use to God at all."

I protested, "Now wait a minute. I don't agree with that. I belong to the Lord, sick or well."

She looked at me skeptically. "If you had more faith, you could *walk right out of this hospital!*"

"But, I *do* have faith, and it is strong."

Karen cocked her head. "Well, in our house we don't *permit* illness to hang around. Just last week my daughter got the flu and had a fever of 103 degrees."

I nibbled the bait. "And? What happened?"

She smiled. "We prayed, that's what! We prayed that demon *right out of her body!* When we finished she still had a fever, but she made herself get on that school bus anyway."

I grimaced. In my opinion, feverish children don't belong in school. I thought for a moment. "Well, what if your daughter got cancer? Would you let her have surgery or radiation?"

Karen hesitated, "H'm, good question. Never thought of that. Well, I can't say for sure, but the way I feel right now I think we would just *pray that cancer away!*" She pranced out the door.

I was shaken. Was my faith too weak? Was I worth healing? I fought back the tears.

Later I unburdened these confusing feelings to my husband, John. He reminded me that God is in control and it isn't our place to tell him what to do. We don't make demands of our heavenly Father. Rather, we approach his throne with humility, adding the words, "If it be thy will," to our petitions. We trust him with the outcome.

Have others suggested that your faith doesn't "measure up"? Those insinuations have launched many a guilt trip for serious Christians. We desperately try to "work up enough" faith so that God will answer our prayers favorably. We momentarily "forget" that our faith is a gift from God, that he hears and responds to our prayers regardless of our level of faith.

Perhaps God has miraculously healed you. I don't doubt his ability to do so, but what about the rest of us who are still waiting for healing? It makes us wonder if Jesus plays favorites with his sheep. We love words like *remission, normal,* and *healed.* Even a respite from sickness would be welcome.

Let's back up about two thousand years. When Jesus walked on this earth, everyone who appealed to him for healing received it. "And he healed all their sick" (Matt. 12:15). Through such wondrous signs, the Messiah witnessed to the fact that he was both God and man. These miracles testified to his divinity. He didn't heal people because of their "Olympic-sized" faith, nor did he ever badger them: "Your faith isn't up to standards yet. Keep plugging away at it and look me up in a few weeks. I'll see what I can do."

Now let's discuss some specific examples of biblical healings. Blind Bartimaeus was sitting by a roadside in Jericho when he heard that Jesus was coming through. While the crowd tried to silence him, he cried out, "Jesus, Son of David, have mercy on me!" (Mark 10:47). Later he begged, "Rabbi, I want to see" (v. 51).

Jesus healed him and said, "Go . . . your faith has healed you" (v. 52).

Oh my! Did Christ say that this man's *faith* had made him well? We tremble at these words. Maybe our faith *is* inferior. A simple explanation will eliminate our fears. It's essential to examine this passage in Greek— the original New Testament language. We need only learn two Greek words, *therapeuo,* which means healing, and *sozo,* which means salvation. End of lesson!

In the Greek, Jesus told Bartimaeus, "Your faith has *saved* (*sozo*) you." The Greek word for healing, *therapeuo,* doesn't even appear in this particular passage. The words, "your faith has healed you," are an inaccurate translation of this verse.

That makes a difference, doesn't it? Now relax. Christ was referring to salvation in this case, not healing. Christ saw the faith in this blind man's heart. Bartimaeus knew that Christ was not a trickster, but God's Son. Because of his spiritual sight, Jesus said, "Your faith has saved you." He could have said, "Because you know me for who I really am, salvation is yours."

Now let's consider the account of the healing of the ten lepers detailed in Luke 17. All ten begged, "Jesus, Master, have pity on us!" (v. 13). Christ instructed them to go and show themselves to the priest. "And as they went, they were cleansed" (v. 14). Only one turned back and praised God when he saw that his body was healed.

Jesus asked, "Were not all ten cleansed? Where are the other nine? Was no one found to return and give praise to God except this foreigner?" (vv. 17–18). Then Christ addressed the man kneeling at his feet: "Rise and go; your faith has made you well" (v. 19).

Here we go again. Another guilt trip—until we examine the Greek and discover that Jesus used the word *sozo*, referring to salvation, not healing. Thus, the correct wording for this passage should be: "Your faith has *saved* you."

This Samaritan leper, because he recognized Jesus as the Messiah, reaped everlasting blessings as one of the redeemed. In contrast, the other lepers probably regarded Jesus as a magician and didn't even bother to thank him.

You and I will not escape physical death unless we happen to be alive when the triumphant Christ returns in the clouds. This frail body will be exchanged for a glorified body. Yes, immediate physical healing would be welcome, but it might not happen. Above all, we need spiritual sight, which far surpasses the fleeting benefits of a physical healing. Jesus said, "For judgment I have come into this world, so that the blind will see and those who see will become blind" (John 9:39).

We have something far more splendid than physical healing. Let's rejoice that we will spend eternal life in heaven because we see Jesus as Savior of mankind. Blind, deaf, paralyzed, or otherwise handicapped, believers claim a special inheritance in the Holy City.

Let's imitate Bartimaeus. Scripture says that after his sight was restored, the former blind man "followed Jesus along the road" (Mark 10:52). Why? To worship and adore the King of Kings.

Whether ill or well, let us follow Christ faithfully, giving thanks for the blessings of eternal life. Psalm 37:5 advises, "Commit your way to the LORD; trust in him and he will do this." What will he do? Read on: "He will make your righteousness shine like the dawn, the justice of your cause like the noonday sun" (v. 6).

May we commit these bodies to the Lord, trusting him for the future. With our eyes fixed on Jesus, we shall triumph.

Dear Father, you know how much I want to be well. Each morning I wonder what it would be like to be normal, to be miraculously and instantly healed. You have all power and could easily take away this physical affliction. Yet I remain as I am. Lord, I pray for grace to accept what I cannot change. Increase my spiritual sight. Thank you for the blessing of eternal life. In Jesus' name. Amen.

MEDICAL BILLS ARE GOING TO BANKRUPT US.

"The LORD is my strength and my shield;
my heart trusts in him." : PSALM 28:7

*D*id your heart skip a beat when you discovered
the daily cost of your room? Do you shudder
each time your physician orders another diagnostic test
or special treatment? Are you afraid that you will be
paying hospital and doctor bills for the rest of your life?

During my hospitalizations I had similar concerns. Not long ago I totaled up medical charges from
the past eight years. According to my calculations, I
now own a $46,560 body! Granted, I don't look that
costly, but I'm surprised that our health insurance
company doesn't hire a "hit man" to eliminate me
before I can submit any more expensive claims!

Did I fret about mounting bills? Yes, especially
in view of the fact that, at the time, my husband served
as a vicar to a church. Doctor visits, prescription drugs,
and x-rays were luxury items we couldn't afford. But my
physical health continued to decline in spite of dwin-
dling resources.

One sunny Thursday in May my husband burst through the front door and announced, "I got paid today!"

I barely glanced at the paycheck before complaining. "Do you realize that my medical bills will cause us to go $200.00 in the hole this month?"

He loosened his tie. "Yes, I'm aware of that."

I threw up my arms in despair. "Well? What are we going to do about it?"

My mate slipped the check back into his wallet and turned to me. "God will provide for us. He always has. You worry too much."

I held my tongue but thought, *How can you be so calm? Are you expecting the money to drop from the sky?*

Two days later when I fumbled through our mail, I noticed a small blue envelope. I ripped it open. To my astonishment a check drifted to the carpet. It was made out to us. The amount? Exactly $200.00. My eyes brimmed with tears as I read the enclosed note from dear friends: "We figured you could use some extra cash because of your illness. God bless you."

I was humbled. Oh, what a lack of faith I had shown. God had met our need, after all. And, as my medical bills multiplied during the following weeks, several church members also offered some financial assistance.

I'm ashamed to admit, though, that I didn't give up worrying on a permanent basis. Months later, during another hospital stay, I received notification that I had exceeded the claim limit set by our insurance company.

This is a terrible blow, I thought. *I've got to be released. Now!*

I tried. I failed. I was told that the physicians were too close to a diagnosis. "If you leave now," they warned, "you'll ruin everything. Don't worry about the bills right now."

I worried anyway. All our careful plans were crumbling. My spouse had completed vicarage and was now in his final year of seminary. I had intended to support us by teaching school. Instead, I was battling a relentless disease. For eight consecutive months I had earned exactly nothing. Meanwhile I was racking up medical bills faster than a gambler placing bets in a Vegas casino.

How would we manage this hospital debt? For that matter, how would we pay the rent? I felt guilty. I considered myself a liability to our family.

Again God rescued us. Many Lutheran congregations responded eagerly to our need, including a church that sponsored a huge benefit for my medical expenses. The amount raised was more than our debt so we were doubly blessed. We had the joy of sharing the excess with other Christians faced with astronomical hospital fees.

The Lord met our financial needs in marvelous, unexpected ways. Prior to my illness we had depended on my salary to provide for this one year of schooling. We were now trusting in God's unlimited provision as our dependence on him increased of necessity.

What about your financial dilemma? Maybe no one will organize a fund-raising event to defray costs.

Perhaps you won't get a cent in the mail. When you go home from the hospital, you may not find anything except extra bills stuffed in your mailbox. In addition, you may learn that the roof is leaking, your refrigerator has conked out, and the car needs major repairs. You may feel overwhelmed. You may even question God's love for you. Does he really care about the financial mess that is keeping you awake nights?

Jesus said, "Your Father knows what you need before you ask him" (Matt. 6:8). Before we even approach his throne in prayer, he is intimately familiar with the anxieties that burden our hearts.

Does he care? Of course. Christ reminded his followers, "Look at the birds of the air; they do not sow or reap or store away in barns, and yet your heavenly Father feeds them. Are you not much more valuable than they?" (Matt. 6:26). If God takes care of his creatures that swarm in oceans, creep upon the earth, and soar in the skies, how much more will he provide for man who was made in his image?

Continue to pray about your needs, asking the Lord to help you make wise decisions. You don't have to tackle this financial crisis singlehandedly. Rather, like the psalmist, say, "I will praise the LORD, who counsels me; even at night my heart instructs me" (Ps. 16:7). God enables us to cope with any challenge. We can safely say, "The LORD is my strength and my shield; my heart trusts in him" (28:7).

Each family has to examine its particular situation carefully to find workable solutions. Some choose to remortgage their home and consolidate other debts to save interest. They may even ask creditors to extend a grace period for payments. Many succeed in slashing grocery bills by serving low-cost meals and purchasing fewer convenience foods. Clothing costs, too, can be reduced if garments are handmade or selected at a thrift shop. Families in a financial bind may try to live more modestly by eliminating unnecessary expenses such as cable TV, magazine subscriptions, eating in restaurants, movies, and other nonessentials.

By budgeting frugally, you may be able to pay off all financial obligations in a few months or years. On the other hand, you may not operate "in the black" again during your lifetime. Even so, you can practice faithful stewardship of the available funds.

Remember the widow and her mite? She wasn't struggling to pay off a hospital bill, but she was facing a financial crisis. This poor woman wanted to give an offering to the Lord, but she had nothing but two copper coins. No Social Security check or retirement benefits would be arriving at her doorstep. What did she do? This trusting believer gave it all to God. Jesus said of her, "This poor widow has put more into the treasury than all the others. . . . She, out of her poverty, put in everything—all she had to live on" (Mark 12:43–44). The devout woman had sufficient faith that she had a sufficient God.

Do you ever jokingly regard those medical fees as a "ransom" for your body? Now, think of the ransom actually paid for your soul. Jesus purchased our souls with his blood at Calvary. You and I are already "bought." Regardless of our bank balances, or lack of them, you and I are heirs as believers.

What types of items do we inherit from deceased

relatives? We may receive precious gems, property, bonds, stocks, certificates, and any number of heirlooms. All of these material treasures can perish.

But our inheritance from God "can never perish, spoil or fade—kept in heaven for you, who through faith are shielded by God's power until the coming of the salvation that is ready to be revealed in the last time" (1 Peter 1:4–5).

Isn't that exciting? God keeps this remarkable inheritance for us in heaven until the time appointed by him.

What does your future hold? Perhaps you will regain financial stability. Maybe you won't. Devastating illnesses force some families into bankruptcy. You may even lose your home. Nevertheless, you will remain rich. You will be rich as an heir of the kingdom. That home can never be repossessed!

Dear Father, lately I've spent too much time worrying. I worry about where the money will come from to pay off this horrendous debt. Worry hasn't changed a thing, of course. It gives me headaches, makes me irritable, and robs me of precious sleep. I know that you are concerned about all of my problems, large or small. Well, this is a king-sized problem. I turn this financial crisis over to you. Guide me to make sound decisions. And Lord, I thank you that eternal life is absolutely free. Amen.

IT'S THE WEEKEND AND I'M SO LONELY.

"And surely I am with you always, to the very end of the age."

MATTHEW 28:20

*W*here is everybody? The morning is half gone and no one has reported to extract blood from your veins. It's too calm. You have a sneaking suspicion that everyone has vacated the premises but you. A peek at the calendar confirms that the weekend has arrived.

Harried nurses rush in and out of your room, performing duties so quickly you wonder if they are hurrying to get back to a euchre game. They aren't. A skeleton staff is rapidly covering all bases so their colleagues can enjoy some time off.

Very few tests and x-rays are scheduled for Saturdays and Sundays (except for emergencies), so you have some free time ahead. You may feel like you are marking time, wasting two days in a hospital bed while everyone else is having fun. Unfortunately, there is no time off from your illness. A "leave of absence" from your sick body would be even more welcome.

You notice that fewer patients are pacing the halls. No doubt many participated in the mass exodus that traditionally occurs on Friday evening and Saturday morning. It's true. Patients try to persuade their physician to either:

1. release them
2. supply them with a weekend pass

Obviously, the former is the preferred choice. Men and women who fail at permanent dismissal attempt to get home on a part-time basis. How? Like a soldier applying for furlough, they beg! Even patients encased in body casts have been known to request this coveted pass.

Who can blame them? Wouldn't you like to escape for a while to the sanctuary of your home, where you can munch popcorn, watch TV, and converse with family members?

You are probably too sick to go home right now. Maybe you are in traction or perhaps you're recuperating from major surgery. If you've had your internal organs rearranged in alphabetical order, you're not going anywhere soon.

I identify with the feelings of isolation that you may be experiencing. I recall several lonely days in a hospital a hundred miles from my home. Visitors? Because of the long trip, my loved ones were only able to come once a week. On the other six days I knew my only "visitors" would be the paperboy and the cleaning lady. Both were difficult to lure into conversation.

In similar circumstances other bored patients walk the halls, play on the elevator, or congregate in the patients' lounge. Since I couldn't walk more than a few feet, even those activities were off limits. Instead, I counted the holes in the ceiling tiles, filed my nails, and nervously drummed my fingers as if that would prompt the clock to tick faster. I was impatient for Monday to arrive so I could finish my tests and push for a dismissal.

One dull Saturday, my twenty-third day in University Hospital, I was so lonely I phoned a volunteer every five minutes and asked her to play various Telemed tapes. In search of more appealing entertainment, I thumbed through the TV listings for the hospital's free channel. The programs did not sound stimulating. I'm surprised listings didn't include such choices as "Getting Ahead of Dandruff," "Five Ways to Multiply Your Medical Costs," and "Your Medical Chart and The C.I.A."

How are you coping with this loneliness? Do you feel left out and forgotten, like something misplaced in a file drawer? Maybe you were bunking with a marathon talker who has since packed and departed. You had thought you would enjoy the peace and quiet, but this much "quiet" is deafening. You hear laughter ringing from the hallway and you ache to be a part of the fun. Time drags. You are eager for someone—anyone—to come by for some idle conversation. What can we patients do when facing overwhelming loneliness?

First of all remember that you are not really alone. Jesus said, "Surely I am with you always, to the very end of the age" (Matt. 28:20). Does he promise to be with us "most of the time"? No. He said *always*. For how long? Until the "very end of the age." He maintains loving vigil over his own as long as we breathe. This is the ultimate in intensive care!

The apostle John, forced into exile because of his Christian beliefs, knew this important fact. Banished to the island of Patmos, he lived in solitude, isolated from friends and family. John had been privileged to walk and talk with Jesus and knew that the Son of God would never forsake him. Instead of wallowing in self-pity, John was fruitful. While living on that island, John penned the book of Revelation by inspiration of the Holy Spirit.

Those who believe in Christ are never truly alone. When writing to the church in Thessalonica, Paul admonished the brethren: "Be joyful always; pray continually; give thanks in all circumstances, for this is God's will for you in Christ Jesus" (1 Thess. 5:16–18). Which circumstances? *All* circumstances, even loneliness.

This time is special. Oh, it isn't exactly what you had in mind, I know. But even "this is the day the LORD has made" (Ps. 118:24). The Creator chose to give you another day that can never be spent again. This psalm continues: "Rejoice and be glad in it." You don't have to like illness, but you can focus on the blessings of God's constant care and everlasting love and thank him for the gift of eternal life in heaven. You can adore him for his merciful promises. "From the rising of the sun to the place where it sets, the name of the LORD is to be praised!" (Ps. 113:3). The Lord is worthy of your worship.

In the unplanned hours that stretch ahead, you

can be strengthened and renewed as you study your Bible. Memorize favorite passages and glean new meanings because of your present situation. Pray, write in a spiritual journal, and listen to Christian tapes.

Is it Sunday morning? You probably miss worshiping with your brothers and sisters in Christ at your local church. However, most hospitals provide a small chapel, usually with at least one chaplain to conduct services. Volunteers stand by to escort the patients. Some patients prefer to watch religious programming or desire to have a quiet time of praise and meditation. Personally, I always opt for the bedside devotions. One particular Sunday stands out in my memory.

I had just read a Psalm and was pondering a Scripture passage when I heard music from the hallway. I poked my head out the door and spied an elderly woman strapped in a chair. Alone in the corridor she was lustily singing the words of "Amazing Grace." Quick tears stung my eyes. She belonged to God, and with a joyful heart she was singing his praises.

Father, please change my grumbling to gratitude. I am alive. You've granted me another day on this earth. Thank you, Lord, for promising to be with me always even when I don't acknowledge your presence. Guide me to a wiser stewardship of this time. In the name of Jesus. Amen.

I CAN'T FACE SURGERY.

"My heart is in anguish within me; the terrors of death assail me."

PSALM 55:4

*T*he physician bustled into Room 415 and confronted my roommate. "Well, Hazel, you have gallstones. We'll have to operate in a couple of days."

"But, I don't want surgery," she protested.

"You don't really have a choice. Here, look at these x-rays. See these stones? They have to come out. Besides, you'll feel better once they're gone." He scooped up the x-rays and dashed off to visit another patient.

Hazel began to sob.

When she calmed down I asked, "Do you want to talk about it?"

"I'm afraid," the sixty-year-old woman admitted. "So afraid."

"Why?"

"I'm afraid that, well, that I might die on the operating table." She began to cry again.

"You do believe in God, don't you?" I pressed.

"Yes."

"You can't possibly die unless he permits it. He's in control. You won't go to heaven until he decides it's time for you to be there. Nothing can happen on that operating table that is against his perfect will for you. Besides, heaven will be wonderful, more wonderful than we could ever imagine." I silently prayed for God to enable me to comfort Hazel.

After we chatted some more about God's omnipotence and the promise of everlasting life, Hazel dried her tears. She promptly began to telephone friends and relatives to tell them about her impending surgery.

Another patient on the floor, Cindy, also dreaded her operation, but for a different reason. Sixteen-year-old Cindy had a morbid fear that she would wake up during the operation and feel unbearable pain. That evening, when her anesthesiologist arrived to explain the procedures, Cindy interrupted him. "How many of your patients ever wake up during surgery?"

He was surprised. "Believe me, Cindy, none of my patients ever wake up to watch their own surgery. Don't you worry. I'm going to stay right in that operating room with you the whole time. I promise you won't feel a thing. And you won't wake up until hours later."

Cindy was relieved. Now she could relax and sleep, confident that the anesthesiologist would take good care of her.

The word *surgery* may evoke paralyzing fears in you. Are you afraid that you will die on the operating table? Are you worried about possible disfigurement?

Is it exploratory surgery? That's a tough one to handle. You may be in agony, wondering what surgeons will discover as they probe beneath that fresh incision.

Fear of the unknown strikes terror in our hearts. We don't like to deal with the "what ifs." We doubt our ablity to cope with surgery's final outcome. As we contemplate ways in which our lives might be changed, we are distressed.

Psalm 55:4 may very well sum up our feelings: "My heart is in anguish within me; the terrors of death assail me." We ache for deliverance. We detest the uncertainty, the waiting, and the nightmares. The situation seems intolerable.

Let's assume for a moment that you are slated for surgery in two days. Now, what might the surgeon tell you afterward? Possibilities include the following:

"Good news! Your operation went beautifully and you should be back on your feet in a week or two."

"It was cancer, but we're fairly sure we got it all."

"Surgery was a success. We have every reason to believe that you can lead a normal life."

"Janet, I'm sorry. We had to remove both breasts. The malignancy had spread too far."

Will the surgeon's words cause despair or joy? Obviously you can't answer that yet, but there is One who already knows the outcome. The King of Kings knows all about your future and hears your pleas for help. "He does not ignore the cry of the afflicted" (Ps. 9:12). You need not tremble. Instead, you can proclaim with confidence: "The LORD is with me; I will not be afraid. What can man do to me?" (118:6). God will supply you with all the strength you need to endure this next trial.

If this is a risky operation, you may be facing death. Don't despair. After all, we are all facing death; it's inevitable. The believer can look forward to departure from this body of trouble and pain. Yes, some of us will reach the blessed arms of Jesus earlier than others. Is that a punishment? Of course not. Exquisite joy awaits us in heaven.

"For the perishable must clothe itself with the imperishable" (1 Cor. 15:53). What happens to our mortal nature? It puts on immortality. We will not perish, but will live forever in a glorified body. Later we read, "'Death has been swallowed up in victory. Where, O death, is your victory? Where, O death, is your sting?' The sting of death is sin, and the power of sin is the law. But thanks be to God! He gives us the victory through our Lord Jesus Christ" (vv. 54–57).

What will happen to you during surgery? And afterward, then what? You needn't wrestle with either question. The surgeon's skillful hands will be guided by the Father. If you don't survive, you will be received into everlasting life. Death cannot overcome the child of God. Because Christ conquered death, we are victorious. Our Savior did not stay in that dark tomb but rose to go to his Father.

Jesus promises, "In my Father's house are many rooms; if it were not so, I would have told you. I am going there to prepare a place for you. And if I go and prepare a place for you, I will come back and take you to be with me that you also may be where I am" (John 14:2–3).

Isn't that marvelous? We do have a glimpse of the future, after all. Our heavenly accommodations have been arranged. By his sacrifice, Jesus made it possible for us to dwell in a mansion with God. He prepares a room for us and welcomes us as his honored and beloved guests. Our earthly sufferings will have ceased and we will live forever in a state of bliss.

Surgery tomorrow? May you say with assurance, "I can handle it. I'm not afraid. The God of the Universe is with me."

Heavenly Father, for days now all I can think about is the "Big S." Surgery! What will happen? Will I survive? Will I be disfigured? Will my loved ones withdraw from me? Please release me from these fears. Remind me that you have all power, knowledge, and authority. I place myself in your hands, Father. In Jesus' name. Amen.

IF I STAY HERE ONE MORE DAY, I'LL GO CRAZY!

"Wait for the LORD; be strong and take
heart and wait for the LORD."

PSALM 27:14

*H*ave you been hospitalized so long that you
display symptoms of paranoia? For example, do
you automatically hide in the restroom when a nurse
approaches with a long needle? When you overhear
surgeons whispering outside your door, do you assume
they are plotting an experimental head transplant with
you as their victim?

Don't be alarmed. Institutionalized people face
overwhelming challenges. Even the most stable of us is
tempted, after so long a time, to knot bedsheets
together and catapult out of the window in a daring
attempt to escape.

On my twenty-ninth day as an inmate ... er, I
mean patient, of Why Sneeze Memorial Hospital, I
worried that I had crossed the border from sanity to
insanity. Desperate to go home, I decided to toss out

hints to my doctor. I cleverly (I thought) pinned the dismissal instructions to my bathrobe.

When Dr. Killdare appeared later that day, he made no comment about the papers attached to my blue robe. Worse yet, I forgot what I had done. When he dashed off, I staggered to a chair just outside the door and sank into it, watching strangers enter and exit the elevator. This choice of entertainment alone indicates that I was no longer of sound mind.

Visitors emerging from the elevator stared at me. Something about my left shoulder seemed to fascinate them. I glanced down and understood immediately why they were gawking. The dismissal instructions were flopping from my nightclothes. Embarrassed, I retreated to my bed and ripped off the papers. "Obviously I'm incompetent," I muttered. "I shouldn't be left alone."

I'm not surprised that I had sunk to that point. After all, I had coped with many bizarre incidents since entering the hospital. Once I was awakened at 6:30 a.m. by the sound of male voices drifting down the corridor. The voices continued unabated until 11:00 p.m. I assumed it was two men who had just set a world record for the longest conversation between males ever documented. I was shocked to learn from the nurse that there was just one speaker, a Mr. Shelly, who had been holding an animated conversation with his arm!

Nurse Baker confessed, "All of Mr. Shelly's roommates ask for quick transfers. They say he drives them nuts!" Permissions were granted. Male patients moved in and out of Room 468 faster than young children traffic to the bathroom during a Sunday sermon.

As a patient I also met my share of "floaters," those folks who drift from room to room by necessity or choice. One silver-haired matron had such an unnatural fear of staying in her bed that she ate her meals standing up in the hallway. Her favorite pastime? Talking. Unfortunately, she often woke up other patients in the middle of the night for a nocturnal chat. Some of us politely suggested that this "social butterfly" be given a mild sedative for the purposes of sleep. Ours!

And, of course, as a patient there were the inevitable mix-ups. I often got the wrong meal, a cold meal, or no meal. Once I woke up to see a nurse carting off my water pitcher. "What's going on?" I whispered.

"Orders. You can't have anything to drink after midnight."

I was perplexed. "Why?"

"Your surgery's tomorrow, you know."

My voice rose. "Surgery? I'm not supposed to have surgery." She darted away, checked her source of information, and returned with a fresh container of water. "You're right," she admitted. "I had you confused with someone else."

The next evening my stress level rose considerably when a male patient in the adjoining room became violent. He threw hot coffee on the nurse, cursed, leaped out of bed, and swung his cane at the gals staffing the nurses' station. They ducked for cover and telephoned security in record time. I lay in my bed trembling.

When security guards subdued this character and led him away, I unclenched my fists and relaxed. Once again I asked, "How much longer, Lord? I'm going crazy in this place!"

When you have been hospitalized so long that you automatically write the hospital's address instead of your own on insurance forms, it's time to think seriously about dismissal. How long have you been a patient? Days? Weeks? Whatever the length of your stay, you are probably already eager to go home.

This impatience is natural. We live in an age when people expect immediate gratification. We have instant coffee, instant puddings, frozen dinners, and fast foods. We drive fast, eat fast, and talk fast (if we take the time to converse at all). Computers, calculators, and microwave ovens take the work and wait out of life.

While ill, we demand more of the same. We want quick, easy-to-digest answers to our problems. We want short-order results. I'm surprised that we don't ask our physicians to install drive-through windows at their offices. Such a convenience poses limitations, but we could have vital signs checked and get flu shots with a minimum of effort expended on our part. Our motto seems to be, "Well, if it has to be, let's get it over with as soon as possible."

As Christians we take our concerns about sickness to God in prayer. But then what do we do? We try to put God on our timetable. Our expectations haven't changed. We want answers—our answers—and we want them in a hurry. When answers don't arrive as soon as we expected, discouragement enfolds us like a shroud.

The Bible speaks of ancient believers who had to wait for God's answers too. Abraham was promised descendants numbering more than the stars, but it was decades before Isaac was born to aged Sarah. God fulfilled the promise, but Abraham may have wondered why God was "taking so long."

King David waited upon the Lord as he sought to shelter himself in the caves of Judea, safe from those who were plotting his murder. We don't know when David penned Psalm 13, but perhaps it was during this persecution that he wrote, "How long, O LORD? Will you forget me forever? How long will my enemy triumph over me?" (vv. 1–2).

Hannah waited for years for one prayer to be answered. She had yearned for a son, but she must have wondered if God would ever grant her heart's desire. What joy she must have felt when at last an infant son, Samuel, was born to her.

The psalmist reminds us that we are to wait on the Lord in a certain way. "I waited *patiently* for the LORD" (Ps. 40:1). When I read that word, I begin to squirm. My own patience wears thin, especially when I am hospitalized. Once I deliberately underlined in red all the references to "wait on the Lord" that appear in the Psalms. I was amazed by the number of red marks. Apparently the Lord knew we would need many reminders.

But read on. There is hope. "He turned to me and heard my cry" (v. 1). God is listening to my petitions and yours. He hasn't forgotten us. Let's trust him to resolve the situation in his time and in his way.

Perhaps you feel fainthearted. You doubt that you can endure one more day of this stress. You're right. Alone, you can't. But—and this is important—God *in you* can handle anything. You are properly equipped for this trial. "I can do everything through him who gives me strength" (Phil. 4:13). Everything? Yea, Lord, *everything!*

You can tolerate this hospital stay. The Lord Almighty dwells within you. What greater resource is there?

Dear Father, I feel like my stress level is rising off the charts. I could calm down if I could just get out of this hospital, away from all this confusion. My blood pressure is recorded and monitored constantly, but no one seems to pay much attention to my frustration level. Oh, how I ache to pass through that EXIT door. I need patience, Lord. Please supply me with all that I need. Soon! In Jesus' name. Amen.

MY LIFE WILL NEVER BE THE SAME.

"Jesus Christ is the same yesterday and today and forever." HEBREWS 13:8

*H*arold was solemn as he mechanically stuffed his pajamas into his suitcase. Soon he would be checking out. As he gazed at the snapshots of his wife and grandchildren, a tear trickled down his cheek. What would happen to them? How much longer could he work? Would he and Joann have to sell their home when he quit managing the hardware store?

This fifty-two-year-old man had entered St. Andrew's Hospital for tests. Specialists had just confirmed the diagnosis. Since then Harold felt as if he had been living a nightmare. It began when a neurologist said, "Harold, tests show you have amyotrophic lateral sclerosis."

He stared at the doctor. "Never heard of it. What is it?"

"You might know it as Lou Gehrig's Disease."

Harold's world collapsed. He had seen that movie. Lou Gehrig had died of that disease, hadn't he?

"You mean—it's terminal?" His heart pounded. This had to be a mistake.

The physician looked away and fingered the charts. "There is nothing we can do, but research may provide a cure. Who knows? We can hope." He lowered his head and inched toward the door. "I'm sorry, really, I am." And with that, he was gone.

Since that shock, Harold had functioned like a robot. He didn't believe the verdict, and yet he did. Now he knew the illness wasn't in his head. The future was frightening. Unanswered questions tormented him.

Has a diagnosis shattered your world? You wonder how you'll adapt to changes. Perhaps you are going home without a limb. Maybe your arms and legs are paralyzed after that horrible car accident. If you have a degenerative illness like Harold, you agonize about increased disability. You hadn't counted on this affliction. Not for a minute. You had so many well-thought-out plans for the future. And now this.

A bundle of problems trail us home from the hospital. For example, some patients are concerned about their looks. Their appearance may have been altered by severe burns, baldness, surgical scars, and side effects of treatments. Others are thin from weight loss or puffed up from steroid medications. We fret. *How will others react to me? For that matter, how can I bear to look at myself?*

In contrast, some of us look the picture of health. This is a mixed blessing, possessing its own unique set of problems. Folks may expect us to operate at peak performance because we don't "look" sick. Bystanders chirp, "You look wonderful. You must feel terrific!"

Granted, these "cheerleaders" intend to boost morale. However such comments make us feel alone and misunderstood. Few can identify with the extreme fatigue that robs us of energy.

For example, I cope with rapidly fatiguing muscles. Walking up or down a sloped surface is as challenging as a climb to the pinnacle of Mt. Everest. It is difficult to walk, stand, or sit up. How do I really feel? Old, tired, only slightly more energetic than a corpse.

Now that you are coping with a health crisis, the question "How are you?" triggers painful emotions. Immediately your struggle with illness comes to mind. Perhaps you hesitate to answer because you don't want to be negative and yet cannot honestly parrot back, "Fine."

Because this question has become more of a greeting than an honest inquiry, not many people expect truthful responses. I think if someone replied, "Well, an artery burst and I have only minutes to live," some people would nod and say, "That's nice. I'm glad to hear it!"

We face petty irritations and major upheavals as we adjust to long-term illness. Because we don't always automatically accept our circumstances, we may wrestle with guilt, anger, and depression. And, of course, we are frustrated when an illness drags on day after day with no reprieve. When others gripe about hangnails, sinus congestion, sore toes, and minor surgery, we might even feel a pang of jealousy. *I wish I had that problem. I'd be back to normal in a matter of days.*

Some patients dwell on yesterday. "I loved that job, but I had to quit because of illness," or "I guess my golfing days are over."

Instead, why not praise God for the abilities that remain? "Thank you for the strength to bathe today," or "How wonderful to be able to taste and smell and hear," or "I'm grateful for the extra time I have to pray for others," or "Thank you, Lord, for a mind that still functions."

Try setting attainable goals and pursuing old and new hobbies you can manage within your present limitations. Some study college correspondence courses. Others enjoy reading, painting, crocheting, and various crafts. If I hadn't been ill, this book would not have been written because I would have been teaching. Writing is a realistic goal, something I can work at while lying down.

Setting priorities is essential. With limited stamina, one cannot expect to accomplish tasks with normal energy. Output, naturally, is also affected. Examine your daily routine carefully and whittle away trivia. Save precious strength for the most important chores and events. The term "energy conservation" takes on an entirely different meaning for the chronically ill.

A Scripture verse encourages us: "Be joyful in hope, patient in affliction, faithful in prayer" (Rom. 12:12). What kind of hope? We hope to get well, of course. But this particular passage refers to a hope that is a certainty, not a mere possibility. Jesus Christ, who rose from the dead, is our everlasting hope. This glorious promise of heaven causes us to rejoice. Meanwhile, we pray for patience to endure these temporary afflictions.

Illness may have wreaked havoc with our best-laid plans, but we can be thankful that God never changes. "Jesus Christ is the same yesterday and today and forever" (Heb. 13:8). We don't know what health trials might complicate our lives, but we can depend on the love and help of the almighty Father.

Dear Father, it's so hard to accept this illness. I bristle when I think of the changes it has caused in my life. Enable me to take stock of my remaining abilities as I set new goals. Yesterday is over. I need to live today to its fullest. Above all, I thank you for my future tomorrows in eternity. Then I shall be free. In Jesus' name. Amen.

WHAT FREE MEDICINE?

"A cheerful heart is good medicine."
PROVERBS 17:22

*H*ave you laughed since climbing into that bed? I hope so, but I realize that some circumstances are too painful to elicit laughter. There is nothing humorous about incurable disease, malignancies, and bone marrow transplants.

I'm not suggesting that you giggle your way mindlessly through your hospital stay. After all, we are told that there is "a time to weep and a time to laugh" (Eccl. 3:4). When your nauseous roommate upchucks into the wastebasket, you sympathize. Anything else is inappropriate. However, when you are escorted to your test in a creaking wooden wheelchair so ancient that it looks as if it might have been borrowed from the Smithsonian, you might find some relief in a good chuckle.

Before we discuss the medicinal benefits of laughter, allow me to share some of my own hospital misadventures. My confinement at Lakeside Clinic will serve the purpose. After initial interrogation by the admitting secretary, I was wheeled to Room 415.

A nurse debriefed me, tossed me an ugly gown, and showed me where to stash my belongings. Next, she showed me how to operate the bed controls. I didn't admit that I had witnessed similar demonstrations in other hospitals. Despite these training sessions, though, I never mastered the mechanics of those three amazing buttons.

It sounds so simple. One button raises and lowers the entire mattress. Another raises or lowers the head of the bed. The third performs the same function with the lower half of the bed.

The minute Nurse Nancy left the room, I touched the knobs and accidentally folded myself into the letter S. How did I manage this stunning performance? While trying to raise the head of the mattress, I poked the wrong button and brought up both knees with a jerk. Humiliated, I struggled to reverse the incorrect action. But, in the process, I punched another wrong button and brought up my head with record speed. And that is precisely how I formed the letter S, again and again. I was clearly a "bed-control drop-out."

For variety I made suicidal ascents toward the ceiling or eased the visitors perched on my bed into standing positions. Not intentionally, of course. Call it a talent. Just by the flip of a button, I negotiated the most daring hospital bed maneuvers ever recorded in the history of our state.

Let's leave the complexity of bed controls and move on to the issue of "Call Buttons Vs. TV Controls." Toddlers who cannot yet speak in complete sentences readily comprehend the difference between a call button and the television controls. I failed to match their skill level. When I tried to turn on the TV, I absently punched the call button. A nurse flew into my room. "What do you want?" Hilda demanded abruptly.

"Uh, well, I just wanted to watch TV."

She snapped off the light over my bed. "Well, you hit the call button and here I am."

"I'm sorry." I giggled nervously. She didn't. She slanted me a cool, appraising look and darted out of my sight.

Ashamed of my bungling, I purposefully avoided all equipment more complicated than my toothbrush. I didn't want to wage any more battles with buttons. To my shock, though, I performed an encore of the "Wrong Button Routine" the following day. In my attempt to watch the local news, I accidentally pressed the call button. In barged Hilda. I gasped, shook my head "no," and lunged backward to switch off the light beaming overhead.

Hilda placed both hands on her bulging hips. "I see you still haven't figured out how to turn on the TV," she announced with a smirk. I felt disgraced. To this day I have a feeling that she thinks my I.Q. is a one-digit number.

Days later my sense of humor almost disintegrated during testing procedures. After a particularly offensive test, I wanted to attach a warning label to my body: DO NOT FOLD, BEND, STAPLE, OR OTHERWISE MUTILATE!

Each time I cruised in my wheelchair to a testing area, I had to pass a bold poster that begged, GIVE

BLOOD. I wanted to shout, "I am! Believe me, I am!" When the blood bank got a "quart low" I suspect they summoned a technician and ordered, "Get some from Mrs. Hamer in 415. She'll never know the difference. Besides, she's a heavy contributor."

When the chaplain and his female assistant visited me one day, I had to suppress a giggle, but waited until they piously paced away. The lady minister was grim, as unemotional as an Egyptian sphinx. I had hoped for encouragement, a smile, and a meaningful Bible verse. Instead, I had the feeling that she had come to do an autopsy and was patiently waiting for the body to expire.

People's habits provide a source of amusement. For example, my roommate's husband always delivered her fresh undies and laundered gowns zipped in his brown bowling bag. I couldn't help wondering if he ever got confused. He never lugged a twelve-pound ball to Lakeside Clinic, but had he toted her lacy pink negligee to Sport Bowl Lanes by mistake? The mere thought tickled my funnybone.

And how can patients be solemn when surgeons parade about in those ridiculous green outfits with matching accessories? By the way, don't those doctors look young? I resisted the urge to ask one tall blond intern if he shouldn't be studying for a geometry quiz. And that surgeon who removed my bunkmate's brain tumor looked like he wasn't old enough to have his beginner's permit.

Now let's talk about the benefits of laughter. Proverbs 17:22 admits, "A cheerful heart is good medicine." This "medicine" doesn't cost a cent and we don't have to fuss with prescriptions and complicated insurance forms. For maximum results we must use this "medicine" at frequent intervals and dispense in generous portions.

How does laughter help our bodies? The exercise stimulates heart, abdomen, and lungs and increases circulation. Some researchers believe that laughter may cause the brain to produce endorphins, hormones that reduce pain and discomfort. Because its action is similar to a medication, laughter may be an aid to recovery.

Norman Cousins, editor of the *Saturday Review*, was given a bleak diagnosis in 1964. He designed his own therapy—reading humorous books and watching old comedies. Mr. Cousins claims that belly laughter was almost like an anesthetic, since, after a session of laughter, he could count on about two hours of pain-free sleep.

When we chuckle, we aren't focusing on our illnesses. This temporary reprieve from anxiety is welcome, isn't it? We need a break from the constant stresses that accompany hospitalization. A sense of humor enables us to view life's troubles with divine perspective.

Painful trials are not foreign to Christians. After all, Jesus told his disciples, "In this world you will have trouble. But take heart! I have overcome the world" (John 16:33). Other Scripture verses undergird the importance of gladness. Proverbs 15:13 claims, "A happy heart makes the face cheerful." In that same chapter we are reminded that "the cheerful heart has a continual feast" (v. 15).

Why should we be cheerful? Certainly not because we are enjoying perfect health or financial stability at the moment, though these would be reasons for gratitude. The passage in John assures us that all believers can rejoice *regardless of their individual circumstances.* Why? Because Jesus claimed confidently, "I have overcome the world."

Because of Christ, we have a deep abiding sense of joy even in the midst of tragedy. Maybe you and I cannot laugh at our illnesses. Yet, in a real sense, we will have the last laugh, after all.

While sojourning on this earth, let's view unhappy circumstances from a heavenly perspective. Laughter is contagious. Let's spread it around whenever possible.

Father, I thank you for the gift of laughter. I admit that I haven't found much to giggle about lately, but when I do, I feel better all over. Above all I thank you that I can rejoice in my salvation. Sickness can't alter that fact. For that I am most grateful. In Jesus' name. Amen.

LET'S TALK ABOUT FRINGE BENEFITS.

"Look to the LORD and his strength; seek his face always." : PSALM 105:4

D oug, a city firefighter, thanks God that he injured his leg three years ago. He claims, "It's the best thing that ever happened to me."

I listened skeptically. After all, few folks praise God for splintered limbs. Doug explained that he was so "busy" before this accident that he had resisted his wife's prodding to read the Bible or attend church.

He had set her straight. "Yeah, I believe in God, but I don't have time for that sort of thing right now and I certainly don't have time to be reading any Bible!"

Days later Doug tumbled off a ladder and was shuttled to the hospital emergency room. X-rays showed a fractured femur. Orthopedic surgeons inserted pins in Doug's leg, wrapped it in a cast, and hooked it to traction. As he sprawled in bed, gazing at the ceiling, four words echoed in Doug's memory: "I don't have time." He couldn't use that excuse now. He plucked a Bible from the drawer of his bedside table and began to read. As he read, the Holy Spirit worked a saving faith in Doug's heart. This man reaped spiritual blessings in abundance.

This health crisis had a great fringe benefit for Doug. Now, how about you? Have you found any blessings in your illness? For example, have you discovered that your faith in God is stronger? Faith is strengthened mightily in the hot furnace of adversity. In our darkest hours, when we grope and fumble about in a thick fog that refuses to lift, we beg God for deliverance. We wail, "I cried out to God for help; I cried out to God to hear me. When I was in distress, I sought the Lord" (Ps. 77:1–2). In our helplessness we "seek his face always" (105:4).

In addition to deepening our faith in God, illness often results in other fringe benefits. Mildred Tengbom claims that we become better listeners to what the Lord has to say during those silent hours of illness. In *Why Waste Your Illness?* she says, "Many of us, as we have moved along in life, have begun to turn a deaf ear to the voice of God speaking to us in the deepest recesses of ourselves." Sickness, then, may serve as a spiritual "hearing aid."

Another unexpected dividend of illness is time for introspection. As we probe inwardly, let's seek answers to questions such as the following:

Are my goals for life Christ-centered?

Am I bearing any fruits of the Spirit as listed in Galatians 5?

How can I bear more fruit?

What relationships do I value?

Am I helping this relationship or hurting it by my actions?

Dozens of questions could be added, but you have the idea. In these quiet hours, examine your motives, relationships, and priorities.

Still more dividends can be counted. Now that you don't have to punch a time clock, you may feel less stress. In this reprieve from life's demands, take time to enjoy God's lovely creation.

I'm ashamed to admit it, but when I was healthy, I was on the run constantly and didn't even notice the beauties of nature. Sickness slowed my frantic schedule to a crawl.

Even so, new adventures awaited. That spring when I managed to straggle to the backyard chaise, I marveled at sea gulls slicing the deep blue sky. It was as though these winged creatures were performing their best aerial shows for my pleasure alone. And, in the tall maples, there was more entertainment. Brown squirrels, oblivious of my presence, mimicked monkeys as they played tag, hung by their tails, and mastered high jumps from the tree limbs to the garage roof. One evening I watched spellbound as God painted an exquisite orchid and crimson sunset. I became an avid admirer of God's creation. This was an unexpected dividend of a slower-paced life.

Let's move on to another important benefit— comforting. Right now God is equipping you to comfort others. In past struggles do you remember those people who ministered to you most effectively? It was probably someone who had endured a similar crisis and could understand your suffering.

Let me illustrate by sharing Meg and Bob's story. This young couple lost a baby late in Meg's pregnancy. Their hopes were shattered. They couldn't bear to look at the empty, waiting bassinet. Well-meaning friends tried to console them. Meg's mother kept it light: "Oh, you'll get over it, dear. Besides, you'll have another baby some day." The neighbors chose to ignore the event rather than risk saying "the wrong thing." Bob's dad announced, "It was for the best." All of these reactions magnified their loss.

Then Meg and Bob were visited by the Kendalls, a couple from church. The Kendalls knew just what to do and say. They, too, had lost a child before birth. They were intimately familiar with the wrenching heartbreak that occurs when one's own flesh dies in the womb. The Kendalls offered vital support to the mourning parents.

Perhaps you've experienced similar situations. For example, if you battle chronic disease, you probably draw support from others afflicted with a lasting illness. They've endured many of the same trials. In contrast, your friend who hasn't had anything more complicated than a head cold can't be expected to understand the ups and downs that accompany constant illness.

And Who is the source of all this comfort? "Praise be to the God and Father of our Lord Jesus Christ, the Father of compassion and the God of all comfort, who comforts us in all our troubles, so that we can comfort those in any trouble with the comfort we ourselves have received from God" (2 Cor. 1:3–4). Simply put, God comforts us and we pass it on. Thus, this marvelous healing balm has multiplied effects.

In her book *Affliction,* Edith Schaeffer wrote: "We are assured that the Lord can comfort us, and that the comfort He gives us in specific and varied situations will be used, through us, to bring comfort to someone else. It is a fantastic economy. Our present affliction contains a tremendous possibility for lasting results."

We have touched on several benefits that often result from illness. In addition, sickness reminds us of our mortality. Our earthly stay is a short one. Each day we are moving a little closer to our permanent residence in the New Jerusalem. "Teach us to number our days aright, that we may gain a heart of wisdom" (Ps. 90:12). While we sojourn here, let's make it our aim to increase in the knowledge of God.

In addition, let's draw delight from life's fleeting pleasures—a baby's smile, a warm hug, a dazzling pink and gold sunrise, a bird's early morning melody. By keeping heavenly perspective, we discover new sources of joy. Above all, we rejoice in Christ's gift of eternal life.

With God's help, we might find that our lives are richer than we ever dreamed possible. Even during illness.

O Lord, so often I view this illness as a thorn in my side. And yet, I know that you use the painful events in our lives to mold character and refine faith. Enable me to draw on these spiritual "fringe benefits" with regularity. Thank you, Father. In Jesus' name. Amen.

I'M GOING HOME!

"It was good for me to be afflicted so that I
might learn your decrees."

PSALM 119:71

*F*inally! What joy you feel when the doctor says
those words you've been longing to hear: "I'm
releasing you to go home tomorrow." He mumbles on
about prescriptions and exercise and other nonessentials, but you hear nothing beyond that beautiful
word—*home.* You resist the urge to ask him to drop you
off at your house on his way home from the office. That
would be tacky. Hitchhiking is dangerous and it's too
far to walk. You figure you'll last for twenty-four more
hours.

Home tomorrow! You can hardly wait. You can
sleep in your own bed without worrying that some
confused patient will climb in beside you. No masked
people in strange costumes will hover over your body
like sinister characters in a science fiction movie. You
won't be escorted to the torture chamber (testing area)
for bizarre experiments on your muscles, flesh, and

internal organs. It's almost over. The finish line is in sight.

Don't start your celebration prematurely. I hate to dampen your enthusiasm for "home sweet home," but you still have a major hurdle to overcome. That's right. You must endure those tricky dismissal formalities.

I once became so perplexed by dismissal rules at one clinic that I wrote the following satire as a "guide" to other patients.

> Statistics indicate that most patients eventually get to go home. But each year a few are officially listed as Missing in Action. Why? They failed to follow the proper procedures. Eyewitnesses have sighted these bewildered patients wandering through hospital corridors and trailing behind laundry carts. Their dismissal instructions are faded and torn, but not discarded. No, these brave men and women cling to the hope that they, too, can unravel the confusing directions they clutch to their bosoms.

> According to *Hospital Digest* (July, 1986) a bedraggled female patient crawled to freedom through the main entrance of U.O. Us Medical Center on May 3, 1986. One month earlier she had virtually disappeared after completing only half of the steps necessary for dismissal. The woman, Ima Cummen, was later honored in a

touching ceremony and presented with a bronzed stethoscope.

I admit to exaggerating a bit. All right, I stretched the facts completely out of shape. But it is a fact that some hospitals make dismissal more complicated than admittance. If administrators read my "Dismissal Treatise," they may simplify instructions (or arrest me as a subversive).

Don't fret. You'll eventually unravel the directions and be whisked to freedom in the family automobile. Soon you'll toss your dead bouquets, tuck your nightclothes into a suitcase, and stash get-well cards and trinkets into sacks. (Don't forget the plastic bedpan. Filled with fresh flowers, it makes a unique centerpiece.)

You're not sorry to be leaving this place. Perhaps you feel like a college student who has just completed a grueling week of finals. The pressure is off for a while. You made it. You're a survivor.

As you glance about this germ-free environment with its antiseptic smells, don't forget how God was present with you. Perhaps you encountered the shadow of death within these walls. Maybe you still flinch when you recall how the physician gripped your hand and said, "You have an incurable disease." What a shock! On the other hand, you may have received good news that brought tears of happiness and relief.

Psalm 119:71 provides a unique insight: "It was good for me to be afflicted so that I might learn your decrees." Do you agree? Some of you don't agree at all at this point in your struggle. The pain is too fresh. Too deep. In the future, though, you may remember this hospitalization as a special time of closeness with the Lord.

During times of great tribulation, we cling to his promises like a non-swimmer clutching a life-preserver. We hold God's Word close to our hearts when we feel ourselves "going under" the deep waters of crisis.

But we have God's assurance: "So do not fear, for I am with you; do not be dismayed, for I am your God. I will strengthen you and help you; I will uphold you with my righteous right hand" (Isa. 41:10). Hope is restored by such an encouraging passage. We dare to believe it and pray, "O Lord, let this happen to me as you have said. Uphold me, Father. I'm sinking."

Are his promises to us valid? Absolutely! "The words of the LORD are flawless, like silver refined in a furnace of clay, purified seven times" (Ps. 12:6). Can we trust God to keep his Word to us? When Paul wrote to Titus, he referred to our heavenly Father as "God, who does not lie" (Titus 1:2). Our Creator is faithful and speaks only the truth. He does not break his promises. Therefore we need not be distressed.

What about your future? Will you be entering another hospital or coming back to this one? We groan at the thought. Another medical crisis? Spare me! More surgery? No thanks. Yet, for some chronically ill patients, future hospitalizations are a grim reality.

We don't know what the future holds. Good health can be lost in a moment by disease or accident. Changes are bound to occur. Even this modern hospital with all its sophisticated equipment will fade away.

In contrast, God's Word is permanent. "But the

word of the Lord stands forever" (1 Peter 1:25). What a comfort. God's promises are never amended or subject to an expiration date. His promises aren't reviewed by a governing board and altered according to the current global conditions or worldviews. His Word never changes.

God has accomplished great things for you and me, hasn't he? Oh, we may be disappointed or even heartbroken about events of our hospitalization, but the Lord didn't forsake us. He enabled us to withstand adversity and pledges to see us through tomorrow's trials as well.

We will soon head for the hospital doors marked EXIT. We will pass through that door with gladness and anticipation. Later we will burst through the front doors of our homes to join loved ones.

During our earthly journey we will pass through many doors. We may file through the doors to a new job, to chemotherapy, to surgery, to a mortuary, or to a nursery where we will greet a newborn grandchild. Sadness lurks behind some doors. Behind others, exceeding joy like that of a newly wedded couple celebrating their marriage.

We need not fear what lies beyond these doors because God is with us. "The LORD will watch over your coming and going both now and forevermore" (Ps. 121:8). And the last door? Because of Jesus, we have confidence that the final door unveils the best surprise of all. It opens to heaven, our eternal home.

Go ahead. Pack up. Above all, take God's blessed promises with you wherever you go.

Father, I can hardly wait to go home. I didn't think I could cope with this trial, but with your infinite love and help I endured. I don't want to think about entering another medical facility. Ever! But, I have no knowledge about the future. Enable me to go through the doors of my life with peace. Thank you, Father, for the splendor that awaits beyond the final door. In Jesus' name. Amen.

MY HOSPITAL DIARY

MY HOSPITAL DIARY

_____

_____

_____

_____

_____

_____

_____

_____

_____

_____

_____

_____

_____

_____

_____

_____

_____

_____

_____

_____

_____

_____

_____

MY HOSPITAL DIARY

_____
_____
_____
_____
_____
_____
_____
_____
_____
_____
_____
_____
_____
_____
_____
_____
_____
_____
_____
_____
_____
_____

MY HOSPITAL DIARY

_____
_____
_____
_____
_____
_____
_____
_____
_____
_____
_____
_____
_____
_____
_____
_____
_____
_____
_____
_____
_____
_____
_____
_____
_____

MY HOSPITAL DIARY

MY HOSPITAL DIARY

_____

_____

_____

_____

_____

_____

_____

_____

_____

_____

_____

_____

_____

_____

_____

_____

_____

_____

_____

_____

_____

_____

_____

_____

_____

MY HOSPITAL DIARY

MY HOSPITAL DIARY

MY HOSPITAL DIARY

_____
_____
_____
_____
_____
_____
_____
_____
_____
_____
_____
_____
_____
_____
_____
_____
_____
_____
_____
_____
_____
_____
_____

MY HOSPITAL DIARY